ECONOMIC CATARACTS

A Chronicle of Efforts to Remove the Obstacles
of Urban Community Engagement and Economic Inclusion

ECONOMIC CATARACTS

A Chronicle of Efforts to Remove the Obstacles
of Urban Community Engagement and Economic Inclusion

PRESTON LOVE, JR.

Omaha, NE

Preston Publishing
c/o Concierge Marketing Inc.
4822 South 133rd Street
Omaha, NE 68137
www.PrestonLoveJr.com

Paperback ISBN: 978-0-9964464-1-9
Mobi ISBN: 978-0-9964464-2-6
EPUB ISBN: 978-0-9964464-3-3

Library of Congress data on file with publisher.

Design and production: Concierge Marketing, Inc.

Cover photo by Jason R. Fischer at Surreal Media Lab

Printed in the United States of America.

10   9   8   7   6   5   4

I dedicate this book to my Lord and savior, Jesus Christ; my new bride and beloved wife Martha; to my dear children, Tiffany, Cory, Crystal, Natalie who joined the lord in 2009; dad Preston, Sr.; mother Betty; grandmothers Mexie, Portia and Georgia; son-in-law Ron Parker and his wife Teresa.

Author Statement

"And this is my prayer: that your love may abound more and more in knowledge and depth of insight, [10]so that you may be able to discern what is best and may be pure and blameless for the day of Christ, [11]filled with the fruit of righteousness that comes through Jesus Christ to the glory and praise of God." Philippians 1:9-11

God blessed me from my beginnings with many gifts: intelligence, athleticism, creativity, musical and artistic ability, a loving intact nuclear family, children and more. With those gifts and a bowl of cherries, my early life flourished with accomplishment after accomplishment and the spoils (e.g. money, recognition, and to some degree, celebrity). All of my thanks went to good fortune, good luck and, of course, my greatness. In spite of being raised early in the Church, no thanks to God, none.

God finally shut me down. Stripped me of all of the above—all. I lost the respect of friends, family and community. The devil was overjoyed and actively participated in my demise. I reached the bottom and Satan celebrated an apparent victory over another high profiler, another child of God.

But one day I found Jesus Christ, not by 12 steps (I did try that) but one step, one step toward the belief in Jesus Christ. Since that moment and my acceptance of Jesus as my personal savior, God has slowly restored all that was lost and more, much more. All of my gifts have been restored. Much more has been added: discernment, wisdom, a vocal singing voice, a spiritual help mate in the form of my new wife, Martha, a saint and Holy-Ghost-filled woman of God.

This Book is a testimonial to the power of God.

"Because of who you are I give you Glory"

Contents

INTRODUCTION

Imagine this book as a snapshot, a short scene, in a much longer "movie." The movie itself represents the thirty-five years I have spent as a community and political operative. Although these experiences occurred almost entirely in and around the Black community and throughout the United States, this snapshot is a chronicle of the most recent years in Omaha.

Like any snapshot, you can only see what's in the picture. You don't see what happened before the photo was taken, and you never see the bigger picture. This snapshot in this book, however, does reflect almost all of my experiences in those interwoven threads of community and politics.

The "outtakes" of this movie—the parts you, the audience, may never see—are these. You won't see, except for a few instances, the experiences that led up to and forced a need to capture the here and now and put it on paper. By and large, my life as the son of a legendary jazz player and historian, Preston Love Sr., are not dealt with here. My experiences in bigtime sports (Division I football and track at University of Nebraska, and semi-pro football with the Lincoln Comets football team) are not discussed. My experiences as a pioneer and junior executive with IBM are not part of this narrative.

My experiences as a retail computer pioneer and businessman are not presented. I don't give details of my early entry into politics and governmental management or my rise to organize and run a presidential campaign for the Reverend Jesse Jackson, the first Black man to run for president, in 1984.

I don't tell you about my involvement with the historic rise of Chicago's first Black mayor, Harold Washington, and my role in his career. I don't discuss my ten-year battle with addictions and later commitment to God. You won't hear about my gift as a gospel soloist or my researching, writing, and performing of two one-man shows (one as Adam Clayton Powell). Other than right here, I will not mention about my lifelong experiences with over fifty historical figures and celebrities.

This snapshot begins with my return to my beloved hometown of Omaha, Nebraska, to be with my ailing mother, Betty Love, in 2006 after the death of my famous father, Preston Love Sr. The status of my section of town, North Omaha, where almost all of the fifty thousand African-Americans live in Omaha, was shocking.

I returned home to find massive poverty, high unemployment, educational gaps, high school-dropout rates, shockingly high levels of sexually transmitted diseases, high crime, and daily violence. This book picks up as my level of dissatisfaction reached its boiling point, followed by an increase in the intensity of my involvement in community and political action. The result: an internal cry for leadership and an internal confidence coming from the accumulation of wisdom, which comes from years of God-given experiences.

This book is a compilation of position papers and initiatives directed toward making a difference where a difference is needed. While my story is based in my hometown, there are lessons, there are premises, there are actions, and there is wisdom in these approaches that can apply in every urban setting in America. I offer this snapshot as a framework for others to reference.

The full "movie" of my life will be committed to a book in the near future.

The anchor of this book is my 2014 paper titled "The 10 Reasons African Americans Are Not Engaged in Their Community."

The paper defines my revelation of the core challenge for my African American community as it relates to community engagement, in which voting is a key component and the fights for economic inclusion. There are cataracts on the eyes of leadership in both the majority and minority communities that obstruct the clear view of what economic inclusion can contribute. This paper is the baseline and the reason for this book.

The paper defines the challenge as I see it, and this book is focused on several enhancements to the definition of the challenge. Section II of the book chronicles my attempts to organize and lead efforts toward solutions. I offer the book as a request for confirmation of the challenge and a reference to others who face the same challenges in their communities. What we all face is "Economic Cataracts" covering the eyes of the greater community and the negative economic impact on the urban minority communities. The result is urban community disengagement.

Photo Album

Picture of my mother and father (1953)

Omaha Star - *1964*
Eight African-Americans on the 1964 UNL Husker Team
Top Left: Bob Devaney, Willie Paschall, Ted Vactor, Harry Wilson
Bottom Left: Preston Love, Tony Jeter, James Brown,
Langston Coleman, Freeman White

Huskers Ron Moore and Preston Love skim hurdles.

Running hurdles at UNL

By MIKE BAXTER

Well-dressed, college-educated Preston Love is a young Lincoln life insurance agent.

He is also a Negro.

Because of his race, the former University of Nebraska athlete said, he has been unable to find the type of housing he wants and can afford.

Graduated last year from NU, Love has been searching for a "real nice" apartment, one with "wall-to-wall carpeting, drapes, furnished with newer furniture."

"If there were not many in town, I can understand where I would have trouble in finding one. But there are a number of them. There are more apartments than people to rent them."

Several of the 15 landlords he spoke to remembered the name Preston Love, outstanding hurdler on the NU track team and a football end.

Nice Area

The Omaha native now lives in T-Town, Lincoln's Negro district running north and south from T Street from about 20th to 27th. He likes the area.

"It's a very nice area," he said. "It's relatively clean, but there are a minimum of extra-nice apartments."

While apartment hunting, he met enough rejections to classify them.

"I was faced with two alternatives. I could telephone and not mention I was a Negro and go out and see the apartment.

"Or I could ask if they have an apartment and tell them that I am a Negro while on the phone and find out their policy right away.

"I did both."

Three Answers

When he did not disclose his race until he appeared at the advertised apartment, he said, he met three reactions:

—There were owners who said "point-blank they didn't like Negroes and didn't want to rent to a Negro."

—Others said they would be "more than happy to rent to a Negro, some of their best friends were Negroes, they knew Negroes in the service, and all that, but people in their place would move out."

Sometimes Love knew most of the persons renting at a particular apartment house, he said, and was confident they would not have moved.

—Some landlords said the apartment had just been rented. "That was the one I hated most. I would call back, giving another voice, and find out it was open again. What affects me most about this is that it's just point-blank telling a lie."

When rejected, "rather than storming out, I'd ask, 'Do you know some place where I can find an apartment?'

"And 103% of the time they'd give you two or three suggestions, every one of them in T-Town."

Love did not seek help from any housing, civil rights or religious group, he said, and he did not consider legal action.

"I hate to put anyone in that position (through court action) even though they put me in a pretty bad one."

Love likes Lincoln, he said, and he likes selling life insurance in Lincoln. "But if I'm going to make my home here, I'd like to have a home."

The veteran of one season with the professional Lincoln Comets football team said his experience has changed his attitude toward civil rights.

"I've never been really a race fighter, a fighter for equality. Now that it has become a problem, I want people to know.

"If someone called me tomorrow and asked me to help (secure equal housing rights), I would agree."

Former Husker at pro football end.

An apartment hunter, Love finds problems.

'No Vacancy' Can Be Said 3 Ways to Negro

Former NU Athlete Finds Excuses Instead of Apartment

Right after my career at UNL

1970 IBM ad from Time Magazine
(ad also used by IBM in the Ebony Magazine*)*

Preston Love, Jr., former Omaha, owner of DATA-MART — America's first home computer and entertainment center.

"If you want to cook with a computer, play a countless variety of games or simply balance your checkbook," said Love, "you'll discover how at DATAMART."

The store is located at 3001 North Fulton Drive, N.E.

"The development of the microcomputers, said Love, "makes it possible for every homeowner and small businessman to enjoy the benefits of an expanding universe of games and the ease of automated record keeping. The computers themselves make possible a whole new dimension in home entertainment and a lifestyle geared to the '70's."

Love, a 1966 economics graduate from the University of Nebraska, joined IBM in October, 1966 and moved rapidly up the executive ladder. In 1972, he was appointed a branch marketing manager with responsibility for over $3 million in annual revenue. The recipient of many national awards for marketing management excellence, Love became, in 1975, the company's Eastern field support manager with responsibility for all of the marketing support efforts for manufacturing customers.

During his years with IBM, Love realized that the next breakthrough in computers would be in the home market. According to Computerworld, an industry trade magazine, the total computer industry is expected to grow from $48.4 billion worldwide in 1977 to $78.2 billion in 1981. Computer sales in the United States grew some 16 per cent in 1977.

Microcomputers are expected to represent 12 per cent of all units sold in the U.S. in 1977, 36 per cent of these to small businesses. By 1981, it is expected that more than 80 per cent of all microcomputers sold will be for home use. In fact, many industry observers, such as Love, feel the home computer will represent the next big thrust in appliance ("brown goods") merchandising, akin to the transistor radio and color T.V.

Love offers a ready explanation, "Owning your own computer is like always having a friend around. If you can read and use a typewriter, you can talk to it and get an answer. And that answer can help you create art, compose music, play a host of games, create your own menus and recipes, balance your checkbook and monitor your home's comfort and security. Some computers even respond to verbal commands. What computers can do is only limited by human imagination."

Datamart Clipping (1980)

12

Preston E. Love Prefers Not to Be 'Out There'

Native Omahan Preston E. Love helped Andrew Young get elected mayor of Atlanta.

The former University of Nebraska-Lincoln football flanker also worked in Harold Washington's campaign for mayor of Chicago and is now deputy campaign manager for the Rev. Jesse Jackson in his bid for the Democratic nomination for president.

A handsome former businessman who is on leave from his job as a department head in the Young administration, Love himself would be a likely candidate for office. But he denied having personal political ambitions.

The 41-year-old son of Omaha jazz musician Preston H. Love said he is more comfortable "behind the scenes. I'm glad I'm not 'out there.' I'm not sure I have what it takes to be a politician. A candidate has to be prepared to make a full-time life commitment. I'm not prepared to do that now. If I can help candidates I agree with, I'm satisfied."

'A Long Shot'

Love, speaking from Jackson campaign headquarters in Washington, granted that the civil rights leader is "a long shot" in the race for the nomination.

"But Jesse has other objectives besides winning the presidency," Love said. "He wants to generate interest in people to register and vote. He wants to help more blacks and Hispanics get elected to city and county offices."

The effort is proving effective, Love said. He cited the registration drive in Mississippi: "Last May only 16,000 blacks and Hispanics were registered in the state. Now there are 50,000. That could make a difference; in the last presidential election, Reagan carried Mississippi by just 11,000 votes."

Computer Expert

Love voices great admiration for Jackson. "I have been working closely with him since summer," he said. "He's extremely intelligent, more so than is generally recognized. I think Jesse is regarded in

Sun Up Interview
By Robert McMorris

some circles as a good speaker without substance. That's an incorrect perception.

"I see him as a brilliant man, very dedicated to what he is doing, working for social justice. Things I've heard about him are quite unfounded. It's exciting to work with him; he generates excitement in everybody around him."

Jackson is drawing on Love's experience in computers to help chart campaign strategies.

Love acquired his computer expertise in his 11 years with the giant International Business Machines Inc. He made good progress working his way up the corporate ladder at IBM, becoming marketing manager for manufacturing before he quit to open a computer store in Atlanta.

"We were sort of pioneers," he Love said, "Our store was one of the first of its kind in the city. I introduced Apple computers to Atlanta."

As director of management systems for Mayor Young, Love is responsible for the city's overall computer operations.

"I met Andy many times over the years, but I never really got to know him until I moved to Atlanta and he resigned as ambassador to the United Nations," Love said. "He's just a unique individual, very visionary. I think he's having a good first administration as mayor. He has instituted a lot of programs that will pay dividends to the city later.

"He was nearly single-handedly responsible for getting the Jimmy Carter Museum for Atlanta. Some residents near the location were against it because

they thought it would disrupt traffic and so forth. If Andy hadn't fought for the museum, it wouldn't have happened."

While at the United Nations, Young frequently made headlines because of his controversial statements. Of those foot-in-mouth tendencies, Love said: "I've worked so closely with Andy I don't notice such things.

"He's inclined to say things that can be taken another way. He doesn't always mean it the way it sounds. Some of the staff don't always know where he's coming from; they're not on his wavelength. Andy's focus is on the vision rather than the day-to-day."

Love indicated that the nation has probably not seen the last of Young because his political aspirations are not necessarily confined to Atlanta.

An Eye-Opener

During Love's days at Omaha Technical High School, he said, his focus was "very much on sports, although I was always a pretty good student." He was an all-state player in football and basketball and was a state champion in high hurdles.

After his graduation from UNL he was drafted by the Detroit Lions, but failed to make the team.

"I was crushed when that happened," he recalled. "But the experience also opened my eyes. The Lions had paid me $1,000 for signing, and if they had kept me on I would have made just $10,000 a year."

He was equipped with a degree in economics and figured he "could do better as an accountant."

His first assignment after joining IBM was in Lincoln. While there, he played one season with a semi-pro football team, the Lincoln Comets.

Today Love stands 6-3 and weighs 200 pounds, about 20 pounds more than in his football days. He and his wife, Camille, have three children.

If Jesse Jackson, in one official capacity or another should go to Washington and ask the former Omahan to go with him, he would probably accept the call. "But I don't have Potomac fever yet," he said. "That's what everybody is afraid of getting. So far I've been too busy to catch it."

OWH *article while living in Atlanta (1984)*

14

In a debate during the Illinois primary in which he won 79 percent of the Black votes, Jesse Jackson maneuvered Walter Mondale (l) and Gary Hart into a fight over who best defends civil rights.

JESSE JACKSON Moves On Up In Bid To Become U.S. President

With campaign adviser Lisa Levine (l), campaign chairman Arnold Pinkney (c) and adviser Preston Love, Jackson tells reporters he is "moving on up" in the race.

By ROBERT E. JOHNSON
JET Associate Publisher

Following a precedent set in 1868 when General Ulysses S. Grant, whose success and fame as a military leader led to his election as President of the United States without ever having held an elective or appointive political office, PUSH President Rev. Jesse Jackson is seeking to parlay his success and fame as a civil rights leader into the U.S. presidency.

He is further emboldened in bid for the nation's highest office

Jet Magazine *(1984)*

During a campaign rally in Washington, D.C., candidate Jackson holds hands of Gary Mayor Richard Hatcher (l) and Washington Mayor Marion Barry, who are among many big city political officials who endorse him.

by also emulating General Dwight David Eisenhower, whose success in leading the Allied armies to victory in Europe during World War II led to his election as the 34th U.S. President, even though he, too, never had been elected or appointed to a political office.

But just as each General Grant and General Eisenhower offered the nation a public record as a warrior who plundered property and conquered people in patriotic service, Jackson is seeking to become chief executive by offering the nation a public record of pushing to save humanity from war, poverty and racism.

Since entering the race on Nov. 3, 1983, he has taken a leave of absence from the Chicago-based human rights organization which he founded in 1971, three years after he was ordained to the ministry of the Baptist faith and four years after Dr. Martin Luther King Jr. appointed him national director of SCLC's Operation Breadbasket.

When the 42-year-old South Carolina-born, North Carolina A&T College-educated and married father of five children decided to seek the nomination of the Democratic Party as its 1984 presidential candidate, it provoked a controversy among Blacks in leadership roles and evoked ecstasy among the Black masses. While some Black leaders, feeling beholden to some of the seven White candidates who announced they were seeking the party's nomination, cautioned that the time was not ripe for a Black to run for President and confided that Jackson was not their choice anyway, the Black masses were asking this

North Omaha Development Envisioned

1991

By Mary de Zutter
World-Herald Staff Writer

Preston Love Jr., a north Omaha resident who has been active in voter registration drives and issues of minority employment, said he wants to put together a blue-ribbon commission to create a development plan and timetable for north Omaha.

County Commissioner Mike Albert said he is ready to back the idea.

"I gave him my support for the commission," Albert said Tuesday after meeting with Love and fellow activist Carole Woods Harris to discuss issues, including county employment of minorities.

"Carole and Preston seem to have a very sincere desire to be a focal point for coordinating a vision of the future for that community, and I applaud them for that," Albert said.

Ms. Harris is on the board of the United Methodist Community Center.

Waiting for Details

Love, whose background includes positions in Jesse Jackson's political campaigns, said he has no intention of seeking office but thinks he can be a catalyst for progress.

Love said he has broached the commission idea with Gov. Nelson, C.R. "Bob" Bell of the Greater Omaha Chamber of Commerce, Mayor Morgan's chief of staff, Paul Welday, and representatives of financial institutions.

"I have been given strong indications that they want to be part of it," though most are awaiting details before making commitments, he said.

Love said he wants a commission including government officials, business leaders and community activists.

He wants the group to develop an "action plan and timetable" for development in north Omaha that might include bringing in a nationally known developer to create tourist attractions in what is now a decaying area.

Love said he would like to see a "Northroads" shopping center, or perhaps a lake on Lake Street. The idea of building new tourist attractions has worked in decaying areas of Baltimore and Atlanta, he said.

The action plan should include government-arranged development incentives, Love said. But it should also address issues of health care, housing, crime and the perception of crime.

"It should include the whole panorama," Love said. "You cannot just build brick and mortar and expect it to work."

Roles of Blacks

While the commission idea was discussed in Love's meeting Tuesday with Douglas County officials, much of the conversation there centered on ways to increase the roles of black people and black-owned businesses in county operations.

Love and Ms. Harris met for an hour with Albert and County Commissioner Howard Buffett. County staff members, including those responsible for purchasing and personnel programs, also attended the meeting at the City-County Building.

The meeting came after an exchange of statements, sometimes confrontational, between Love and Buffett during the past few months.

The meeting "was a major positive step," Love said. "I think we made some positive movements to really begin to open up some channels, both in minority hiring at all levels and in the use of minority businesses in a number of ways."

Buffett caught a plane shortly after the meeting. Calling that evening from

Please turn to Page 17, Col. 4

North Omaha Development Envisioned

● Continued from Page 11

California, he said the session was productive. He said he will be interested to see if Love can turn away from his formerly confrontational approach and begin to work together with county officials who share his goals of increased opportunities for blacks.

Albert said the discussion was good. "Everybody came away from the meeting with a positive attitude toward the future," he said.

Since January, Buffett and Love have discussed county government's inclusion of minority group members. They have disagreed in speeches. In written correspondence, they have sought each other's help in moving the county toward its affirmative action goals.

In the Tuesday meeting, the commissioners and the community activists agreed to join hands on the next step at the county level. They will jointly invite all county elected officials to a meeting on minority inclusion, which will probably be next month. The elected officials, such as the county assessor, sheriff, clerk and engineer, run their own departments and are outside the direct control of the County Board.

An analysis of Douglas County employment figures indicated that these elected officials, as a group, hire significantly fewer minorities than do departments under the control of the County Board.

Another decision coming from Tuesday's meeting, Love said, is that he and a number of volunteers who are part of his North Omaha Community Advocacy Network will begin to distribute information about future county contracts and bidding procedures in order to increase the number of minority firms in the bidding.

OWH *article while living in Atlanta (1991)*

18

* * *

Atlanta Love Note

Hello! Here's a familiar name: Preston Love.

In Time magazine's cover story on prospective presidential candidate Jesse Jackson, reference is made to "a wealth of first-rate black political pros Jackson can draw on." Among them: "Preston Love, a top official under Mayor (Andrew) Young in Atlanta."

Time was talking about **Preston Edwin Love**, 41, Omaha native and eldest son of **Preston Haynes Love**, jazz musician and author of the "Love Notes" column which appears frequently in The World-Herald.

Love, the younger, is remembered by sports fans as a three-sport all-stater at Tech High School who later played flanker for Bob Devaney at the University of Nebraska.

In Young Campaign

Proud Papa said Preston Edwin was with IBM for 11 years after graduating from Nebraska, living in various cities while making his way up the management ladder. "He was doing very well with IBM, but he wanted to go into business for himself, so he started his own computer company in Atlanta," his father said.

He said his son worked in Young's successful campaign for mayor, later

Robert McMorris

joining the administration as budget finance director. He is now director of the office of management systems.

'Computerized' Race

The elder Love said Mayor Young told him his son played a key role in getting him elected by "computerizing" his campaign.

Preston Edwin was given a leave of absence to lend his computer expertise to Harold Washington's successful campaign for mayor of Chicago and is now similarly advising Jackson. The two were recently pictured in a Page 1 photo in the Los Angeles Times.

The senior Love said he doesn't think his son plans to run for office himself: "I think he's happy just being a king maker."

* * *

McMorris article

Preston Love Jr. 1992
Candidate for M.U.D.

Preston Love Jr.

Preston Love Jr., advocate for North Omaha and increased voter participation, has thrown his hat in the ring for the Board of M.U.D. The M.U.D. election is nonpartisan and at-large. The board has seven members and is responsible for policy relating to the city's gas and water operations. M.U.D. has a $185 million budget in 1992 and recently increased gas rates by 2%.

Preston listed five reasons for candidacy for M.U.D.

1. To hold down gas and water rates with a special emphasis on protecting our senior citizens.

2. To aggressively provide leadership in the protection and deve-lopment of our drinking water, at the source, during treatment and including our distribution systems.

3. To provide for increased participation of minorities in employment and promotion at M.U.D.

4. To establish new and effective programs for M.U.D. to purchase from Omaha and minority businesses.

5. To look for ways to better manage the M.U.D. operations, including people, operations and spending.

Preston urged people to register to vote, support he and other candidates who have the interest of community as central to their public service. The election is May 12th. Cliff Groves is Chairman of the Committee to Elect Preston Love to M.U.D. People interested in supporting his candidacy can call 691-8170.

MUD candidate

*2008 leadership Award–winning Caucus training.
Led to the historic Nebraska split electoral vote*

*Me in 2012 while organizing for Obama in Columbus,
Ohio with actress Traci Ross (Singer Diana Ross's daughter).*

COMMUNITY CONNECTION

D | NORTHWEST METRO | OMAHA WORLD-HERALD SATURDAY, FEBRUARY 27, 2010 OMAHA.COM

Club founded on hunger for more information

Preston Love Jr. opens the Hungry Club lunch at Big Mama's Kitchen. The group normally meets monthly but met weekly during February for Black History Month.

KILEY CRUSE/THE WORLD-HERALD

■ The Hungry Club regularly fills Big Mama's Kitchen for its monthly meetings.

By JOHN KEENAN
WORLD-HERALD STAFF WRITER

Preston Love Jr. is playing to the crowd.

As he addresses about 50 diners at Big Mama's Kitchen in north Omaha, Love is jazzed, jittering around a cleared-out area with a microphone in his hand, briefly crooning a song, calling out greetings to the people he recognizes — City Councilman Ben Gray, actor John Beasley.

"When they get here early, I mess with them," he confides to a diner.

He steps over to a table of newcomers, a party from Big Brothers Big Sisters of the Midlands, gets their names and introduces them to the group at large. Then he praises the organization for the good work it does in the community.

Love is hosting the latest meeting of the Hungry Club, a community-based social lunch group that he formed about two years ago.

"It's one of those things where I was just laying in bed watching TV and said, 'You know ...'" Love recalls.

"The real reason that I started thinking about it was the ... lack of a lot of ways for us to communicate in north Omaha about things going on," he said. "We have the Omaha Star, and we had at the time Channel 22, really that was all we had."

Now, they have the Hungry Club.

The club, which usually meets on the first Wednesday of each month, spent February marking Black History Month with weekly events that included a preview of "Jitney" at the John Beasley Theater; a history of the Omaha Star and its founder, Mildred Brown; and Love himself performing a one-man show as Adam Clayton Powell.

"I thought the community was hungry for more information, so that's the idea; hungry for information and hungry for a good meal

See Hungry: Page 2

Hungry Club

Hungry: Club offers connection to community

Continued from Page 1

is where the name comes from. It has really turned out to be just a great deal," Love said.

In April, it will have been two years.

"Preston came to us when we opened," said Patricia Barron, owner of Big Mama's Kitchen on the Turning Point campus, which has hosted the club since its inception. Attendance initially was slow, she said, but grew to the point where the restaurant is usually close to full for the monthly events.

"It's brought people from all over, outside the community and inside the community," she said. "And we're happy about that.

"Preston does things for the community, and we're trying to do something for the community," Barron said, explaining why the venue and the club have been a good match.

"Plus, I think our community is hungry for information, and this is one resource where it can come and hear and see what's being done in the community or proposed for the community."

As the prestige of the club has grown, Love has also found it easier to schedule guests. Actor Beasley and U.S. Rep. Lee Terry were two high-profile visitors in February.

"Now, getting a speaker, it takes me three minutes a month," Love said. "I've got so many options, and people call me now."

Diane Perry, at the club for the presentation on Brown, said the Hungry Club provides a connection to the community.

"I like the diversity of the programs, the speakers that they bring in," she said. "And it helps me establish relationships with individuals, so I can learn more about the community and be a part of it."

That's one of the club's goals, Love said.

"One thing that has turned out to be a big part of the Hungry Club is networking," he said. "And now I force it; I make people go across and greet other folk. There's both social and business networking going on there."

Contact the writer:
444-1074, john.keenan@owh.com

Second half of article from page 21

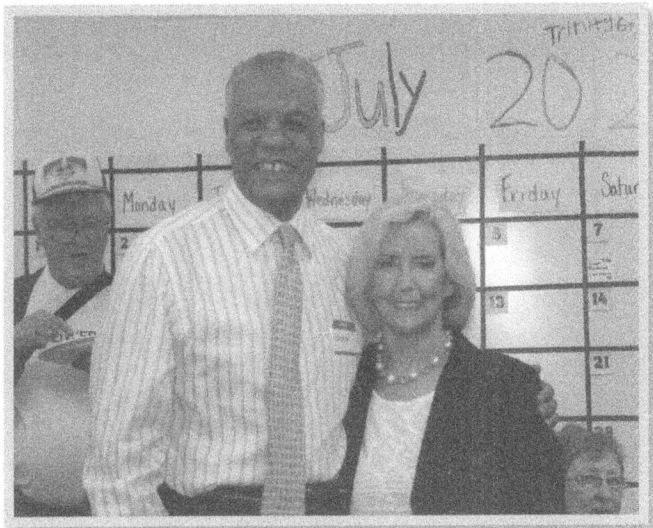

Me with Lilly Ledbetter (Obama's first signed law as President was an equal pay for women bill named the Ledbetter law because she was an activist for equal pay) in Columbus, Ohio, while working for the Obama Campaign in 2012.

Leadership farewell dinner in my honor from my organizational efforts for Obama in Columbus, Ohio (2012)

Poster from one of my Powell performances (playwright and performer)

Preston Love Jr.

Presents

"Stories and Experiences: From Cotton Bowl to Cotton Candy"

Preston Love Jr. after turning 70 years old in 2012, began reflecting on the very unique life experiences he has had. After his highly acclaimed one man performance (as Adam Clayton Powell) that he researched, wrote and performs, Preston has again written a captivating one man performance. This performance will chronicle his interaction and involvement with many historical events, celebrity and historic individuals, and his life's highs and lows. The stories will entertain you, make you laugh, make you cry, make you think and make you say wow!!!. The performance will include music by keyboard artist Orville Johnson.
The performance will conclude with audience Q&A regarding stories from the vast list of personalities below.

This is not a verbal resume, this performance will tell incredible behind the scene stories from his experiences including; Bob Devaney (NU Football Coach); IBM's first experiment with Black professionals; the Atlanta civil rights families including Coretta King; his organization, management and daily interaction with Presidential candidate Jesse Jackson Sr.; his miracle near death experiences with a horse and with drugs.

If you think you know Preston you don't, if you think you know your neighbor you don't there is more; "the rest of the story".

Personalities Preston has **known personally** and has stories, include:

Harold Washington	Shirley Franklin	John Beasley
Clark Terry	Bill Cambell	Anatoly Dobrynin, (Soviet
Count Basie	Mary Barry	Ambassador to the United
Jesse Jackson Sr.	Coleman Young	Nations)
Jesse Jackson Jr.	Smokey Robinson	Preston Love Sr
Richard Hatcher	Dr J	Minister Louis Farrakhan
Ara Parseghian	Jim Marshall	Ron Brown
Bob Devaney	Robert Johnson	Walter Fauntroy
Tom Osborne	Coretta King	Marla Gibbs
Maya Angelou	Gayle Sayers	Jesus Christ
John Lewis	Bob Boozer	Paul Silas
Julian Bond	Ernie Chambers	Hosea Williams
Johnny Otis	Bob Gibson	Buddy Miles
Andrew Young	Johnny Rodgers	Lester Abrams
Bill Cosby	Lynn Moody	Calvin Keys
James Baldwin	Hugh Hefner	Mildred Brown
Maynard Jackson	Alexis Herman	Marion Barry
Charlie Rose	Charlayne Hunter-Gault	Kathy Hughes

Poster for my second written performance (playwright and performer)

With three Heisman Trophy winners including friend Johnny Rodgers

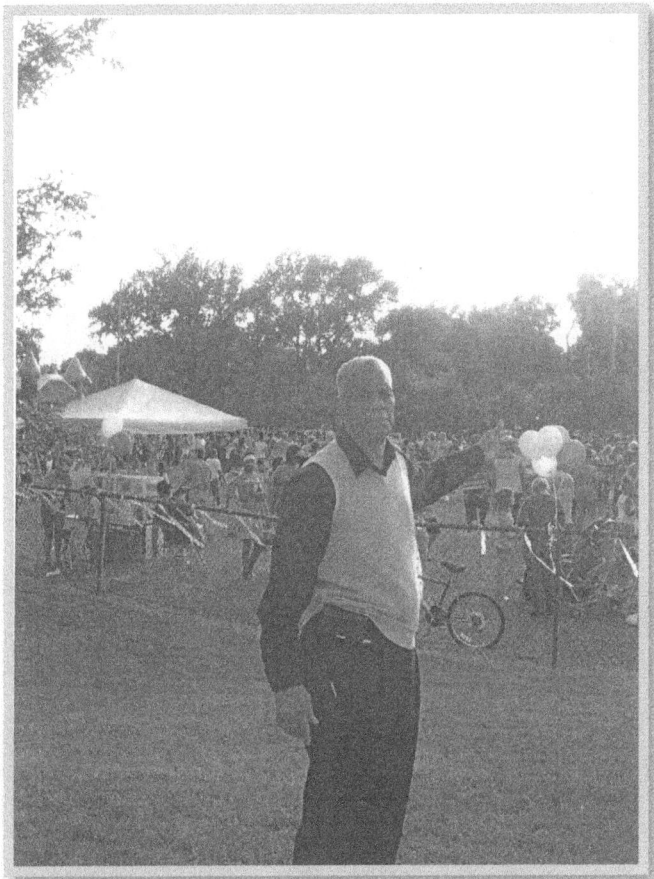

Doing voter registration at a 2014 ABIDE Network block party (1500 attendees)

LOCAL NEWS

Preston Love Jr. Joins Senate Candidate's Staff

U.S. Senate candidate Dave Domina has hired experienced political activist Preston Love Jr. to advise him on north Omaha needs and to coordinate election efforts for Nebraska's second Congressional District.

Dave Domina is convinced the nation needs a powerful, clear voice, and an objective, nonpartisan mind from Nebraska in the Senate. Domina is among Nebraska's most experienced courtroom lawyers. He handled 2 of 3 impeachment cases in Nebraska history, and has been involved in most of the State's highly visible courtroom dramas for decades.

Domina is from a farm background in Coleridge in Cedar County. His considerable service to farmers and ranchers foretell a strong race in the Third District and therefore a substantial chance for success in the campaign.

Domina's campaign focus is upon restoration of the middle class, and eliminating unfair taxation, trade, and spending policies geared to huge corporations and unfair trade that cost the nation jobs and small business opportunities daily. Domina believes correcting these two problems are basic to job creation, the economy and the economic future of all. He stresses that the U.S. cannot be safe unless it can keep its government open for business, live within its budget, and pay its bills while caring for its people. Domina is committed to the growth of north Omaha including the development of jobs.

Love informed the Omaha Star that while he has been active in many political efforts, he never joins the staff of any campaign he does not fully

Love   Domina

believe in. Love stated "Never would I join a local campaign if I didn't believe that the candidate was good for north Omaha. Dave Domina has a great chance of winning and when he does north Omaha will finally have positive federal representation that enhances our views and needs." Preston says he hopes north Omaha will vote in record numbers in 2014 and looks forward to the community getting to know Domina.

Domina announcement

Speaking to Omaha stop of national bus traveling the USA for Middle Class (2014)

With Dave Domina and wife Carol at my wedding (wife Martha) April 2014

Community meeting with deputy campaign manager for US Senate candidate Dave Domina, along with City Councilman Ben Gray and senior citizens

With students from Nathan Hale Middle School. It was a great civic education event

Hope Center youth after I presented and provided a tour of North Omaha

Singing praise to the Lord (Kansas City, MO)

10 REASONS AFRICAN-AMERICANS ARE NOT ENGAGED IN THEIR COMMUNITY

Plainly and simply, African-Americans are not voting. Why should they? Because they can make a difference, promote the change they wish, and become engaged in the workings of their communities.

In my beloved hometown of Omaha and, in particular North Omaha, where 80 percent of the African-American population lives (numbering some fifty thousand people), my North Omaha community is currently suffering from most, if not all, of the ills of a minority-based urban community.

We are disengaged from the community at a time when the buzzword is *engagement*.

The issues are no surprise: high poverty, high unemployment, educational gaps, health care disparities, violence, drugs, and crime subcultures and more. Add to that the lack of real Economic Inclusion in the public and private sectors. My focus is the effect these

factors have on our voter turnout. Let me give
you some of the numbers for North Omaha:

> 2004 Presidential election: we voted
> at 44% while the rest of the county
> voted at 65%—a 21% gap.

> 2008 Obama first election: we voted
> at 62% while the rest of the county
> voted at 72%—a 10% gap.

> 2009 City council: we voted at 23%
> while the rest of the county voted at
> 27%—a 4% gap.

> 2012 Obama second election: we
> voted at 55% while the rest of the
> county voted at 68%—a 13% gap.

> 2014 Senate/House/Governor: we
> voted 30% while the rest of the county
> voted at 44%—a 13% gap.

Even when we African-Americans had the
opportunity to vote for an African-American
for President, we still were outvoted (with a low
turnout) in 2008 and again in 2012 at gaps of 10
percent and 13 percent, respectively.

Let me give you a historic frame of reference.
In 1983 when Harold Washington ran and won
as the first Black mayor of Chicago, the overall

turnout in the African-American community was over 90 percent. So a 30 percent voter turnout is not only lower, it's critically low.

Additionally, if you remove the votes cast by our Black senior citizens, then turnout percentages in North Omaha would be even lower because that part of our community votes.

After watching and participating in the political community for nearly thirty-five years, I offer the following reasons why African-Americans are not voting.

10 Reasons African-Americans Are Not Voting

1. **Poverty.** Poverty, unemployment, and all of its residuals are at the top of the list. Poor people are overwhelmed, overburdened, and removed from the mainstream because they are strictly trying to survive and fighting hopelessness. Additionally, in their minds, the system has failed them. Their focus in life places voting at the bottom of their personal agendas. While many of us realize that voting could assist in changing their plight, it is a difficult sell to the poor. We can make a major impact

on voting by building some wealth in North Omaha. Jobs, contracts, selling of goods and services, and construction jobs need to increase. This is where the case for Economic Inclusion collides with voting. We build wealth by aggressive and focused inclusion. When our urban communities get relief from the survival mode, they will begin to become more engaged in a full range of community issues; neighborhood, education, civic and social organizations, volunteerism and voting.

2. **Cultural disconnect.** There is a strong percentage of people in our current African-American community who are living in an alternate economy: they are involved in drug sales, crime, and the resulting violence. That culture is in full-fledged operation and is disconnected from our mainstream culture (such as church, lawfulness, African-American culture, music, arts, and community development) and definitely not voting. This culture is not there because of some DNA flaw, but rather because poverty and lack of opportunity has elbowed them into a world of alternate survival. The world

works for them. Until we provide better alternatives, they will stay in poverty. We provide the alternative via jobs, contracts, small business development. By the way, that's Economic Inclusion. When we offer those alternatives, many will migrate back to the mainstream and community engagement—and ultimately, participation in the voting process.

3. **Failure of representation.** Reduction of responsible, accountable, and focused representation is a growing problem. Because of our lack of votes, most of our elected officials are elected with few actual votes. That's our fault. There are exceptions, but many of our elected officials are absent in the heavy lifting for the fight for a better community via voter turnout. This effort should be more of a leadership team effort, but it is not. By and large, our leaders and elected officials are not involved in the workings and hard work to get out our community vote. Additionally, we are heavy with numerous nonprofits. The good news is that they are doing great things with and for North Omaha. The bad news is that

there is an overabundance of non-profits
compared to for-profits, and that creates a
strange community culture. A culture that
does not support itself. It's a community
that is supported by outside money. These
nonprofits are overly afraid to do much, in
fear of losing their 501(c)(3) status and the
foundation dollars. They are afraid of getting
out of favor with their funding sources, or,
in the case of the leadership, their jobs. I
can respect that but in most cases the fears
are overstated. We are left with few to carry
the banner for the critical and controversial
issues of our community. Most importantly,
issues affecting our community are partisan
and/or personality based. That is a hurdle
the non-profits are not willing to tackle.
The result is no leadership on the critical
voting issues, leading to a stunted voting
component.

4. **Return of Jim Crow.** First a definition.
    Named after a stereotypical minstrel show,
    Jim Crow came to describe government-
    sanctioned racial discrimination such as
    separate drinking fountains for "colored"
    and "white."

Currently, our community votes predominantly Democratic. At the height of the Jim Crow era, our community was faced with a number of impediments to voting, directed to retard the vote of Blacks:

- the poll tax (a creative measure to require a potential voter to provide money to register and/or vote)

- gerrymandering (creating voting districts to highly favor White candidates or party, minimizing the power effect of large Black blocs of votes)

- literacy tests (requiring a most unreasonable test prior to being allowed to register/vote. Example: reciting the Preamble to the Constitution from memory and without error)

- grandfather clauses (laughable requirement that a voter whose grandfather voted would be allowed to register/vote. This, of course, automatically eliminated Black voters whose grandfathers were prohibited from voting), and

- intimidation including violence and killing.

The 1965 Voting Rights Act made a major dent in these efforts to curb Black voting, and as result Black voter participation increased significantly. Today the enemy to Black voter participation returns in the form of numerous new and old voter impediments. Voter ID laws, rampant voter purges, selected and targeted removal of "early voting" conveniences, redistricting, gerrymandering, ex-offender voter denial, fraud, and manipulative measures like the poll closing shenanigans in 2012 by the Douglas County election Commission.

In the 2008 presidential Election Blacks voted heavily primarily because of the candidacy of Barack Obama. With minimal analysis one could easily determine where the votes came from. In Douglas County, those votes came from North Omaha. Several precincts had extremely low voter turnout. In 2012 the Election commission shockingly closed over half of the polling places in North Omaha. That resulted in mass confusion and total loss of confidence in the "system." In addition, letters were sent to one of the high-turnout precincts, telling voters to go vote at a polling place that was actually closed. In another case, voters who lived in high rise public housing and who had polling places in their own buildings were directed to vote in far off locations. Voters were confused, and the result was a low voter turnout. I led efforts by my community and was able to restore half of the closed polling places, but the damage to voter confidence and the resulting mistrust lingers. That's the New Jim Crow.

5. **Lack of understanding of the power and leverage of voting.** North Omaha is a separate and distinct community. Not unified but a voting bloc, nonetheless. Voting blocs have power. They have the power to determine outcomes in important elections. That power emanates from the campaigns and candidates who clearly understand the power of voting blocs. A voting bloc (a unit with a common purpose) can demand recognition of its issues, pro and con, can demand representation, and can be expected to be rewarded for their loyalty to campaigns and candidates. When the leadership of the voting blocs rises to

fight for the voting bloc communities, that leader has leverage if he or she has a strong voting bloc. If leadership is not strong, there is no power, there is no leverage. This is a classic chicken and egg scenario. Is the leadership not strong because the vote is not strong or is the vote not strong because the leadership is not strong. Help!! The answer: grow a roster, strong leadership will build a strong vote.

6. **Failure to connect voting to our lives.** One of the most frequent comments I hear from a potential voter is that "my vote does not matter." This is also one of my most difficult arguments for I often fear that I cannot quickly articulate a short sound bite that would change their minds, because every vote does matter. Take the now high-profile community of Ferguson, Missouri: population 22,000, 67 percent African-American, high poverty, double-digit unemployment. The citizens of Ferguson have the power to singlehandedly elect the mayor (which includes the appointment of the police chief). They have the power to singlehandedly elect most of the city

council and school board and other
boards. Yet what do the facts reveal? White
mayor, White police chief, five White city
council members, one Black, and of the
six members of the school board, only one
is Black. On the police force, of fifty-three
officers, only three are Black. Why? Because
Blacks in Ferguson voted at 8 percent in the
last mayoral race. Their votes could have
changed the tragic history we see playing
out today. I deal with this further later in
"10 Reasons Why Nonvoters Should Vote".

7. **Lack of coalitions and unity.** North Omaha
suffers from the rampant level of disunity
in every direction. Wealthy Omaha is by no
means in sync with poverty-stricken North
Omaha. Racism is alive and well, albeit well
disguised. There is little unity between North
Omaha and other parts of the city. There
is an arm's length between North Omaha
and its newer residents (Latino, Asians and
Sudanese, for example). In spite of the obvious
advantages of a coalition between north and
south Omaha for common purposes and
some meager attempts, that coalition also
suffers. Foremost there is a total disconnect

within the Black leadership. We don't have the luxury of being fractionalized. We need to be a collective force, but we are not. We are lacking a common ground among our leadership, which is hurting us and undermining our community effectiveness. We lack the power of making coalitions with other voting blocs, which would increase our leverage. Where there is no unity, the community becomes confused, and a confused community will not vote.

8. **Need for increased civic education.** Education about the functions of the branches of government at the local, county, state, and federal levels needs to be increased. Elementary, middle school, and high school students should have stronger civic-related education. This will increase voter participation at all levels related to voting—voter self-education, voter registration, volunteering, and voting. So many don't know who or what is on the ballot and what's at stake. A more informed community will vote. There is a need for proactive initiatives directed to this issue. Collaborative programs with schools and

youth and adult groups, all directed to increased civic knowledge at every level is critical going forward.

9. **Big money.** Big money has changed electoral politics to the detriment of campaigns that don't have access to it. This almost unlimited access to cash by non-urban based and supported candidates does the obvious: it puts urban communities at an almost insurmountable disadvantage. In the 2014 election for US Senate in Nebraska, the Republican outspent the Democrat by five to one, raising $5 million mostly from outside Big Money interests. Voters are now realizing all over this country that if Big Money is behind a campaign, it will be very hard to overcome. If you know an important race or issue is going to be bought, you are less likely to go to the polls.

10. **God.** People with strong core values and beliefs vote. Churchgoers are far more likely to vote than non-churchgoers. Use of prayer to address all of our ills need not be overlooked here. I believe in the power of God to overcome all cataracts. First we must have faith in his power and we must participate with him in his solutions.

It is my view that our greater communities should strive to have clear vision and resolve to deal with the aforementioned problems. It is also my contention that our community leaders have a block (a cataract if you will), blinding their sight of the great value of fully engaged urban communities. Just to mention a view values: lower crime and violence, stakeholders in the greater growth, reduction in the costs of poverty (prison courts, property devaluation, complete disengagement in community).

Now what?

Each of us who is concerned about these trends needs to review this list of ten reasons why African-Americans are not engaged, and then go about the business of developing plans and programs that can positively impact one or more of these impediments. Section 2 of this book captures some of my efforts to remove the obstacles mentioned above.

These ten reasons apply not just to Omaha, Nebraska, or Ferguson, Missouri. They apply to most poor African-American communities in the United States, as well as many Latino communities. To understand this urban disengagement, let's first look at the history.

Section 1:
The History

THE RESIDUALS
OF POVERTY

For years, North Omaha has been in the national ranking as one of the top five urban communities with its residents living in poverty. We also rank high in many other unfortunate categories such as teen unemployment, teen poverty, teen STDs, and on and on. While the national unemployment rate is approximately 7.85 percent and locally reported as an admirable 2.3 percent, unemployment in North Omaha is in the double digits.

Poverty. The key solution to poverty is contracts, jobs. And business opportunities undergirded by education.

With the increase of contracts that results in creating jobs comes a decrease in crime and the many negative residuals with our families and small businesses. Gang violence and lawlessness all are affected when we get jobs, and jobs affect poverty. Simply stated, we need contracts and jobs.

North Omaha Black contractors need contracts in order to create jobs. Providing these contractors with work is critical to this poverty formula and their survival. Black contractors in North Omaha awake daily with the prospect of moving around North Omaha and giving eyewitness to public, private, and nonprofit projects in their own community, with very little, if any, participation.

With few exceptions, such as the city's emerging and small business ordinance and a recent relatively large public works contract (the $2.3 billion CSO project), all parties—public, private, and nonprofit—are guilty of not contracting with Black contractors anywhere in Omaha, but more dramatically not in their own poverty-stricken community. It is an affront to our community and an affront to the contractors.

We have Black contractors who are capable. Capable of building houses, commercial buildings, laying concrete, doing electrical, renovation, roofing, and participating in the nearly $2 billion CSO project. CSO is combined sewer overflow, a major construction project in the city. The project is federally mandated but funded by local citizens, and it is happening mostly in North Omaha. Small contractors do have problems with capacity, raising capital, getting bonding, and obtaining credit. These problems complicate their world, but the real bottom line is they are not getting the opportunities.

Black contractors challenge representatives from the public, private, and nonprofit sectors to come forward and initiate some serious attempts to employ these Black contractors. When spring approaches, work abounds. Black contractors cannot continue to sit idly by while contracting opportunities exist.

While this section deals with the historical development of North Omaha's economic challenges, Section 2 addresses the focus of efforts toward solutions. Let's fast forward for better understanding. In responding to the issue of Black contractors not getting contracts for development in North Omaha, we recently issued the following press alert.

North Omaha Contractors Respond: "Enough is Enough"

Breaking News: North Omaha is a poverty-stricken community. A community surrounded by vast wealth, booming economy, unemployment under 5 percent, aggressive economic growth, and construction.

Breaking News: Where you have poverty, you have exponential crime, sociopathic subcultures, and violence.

Omaha has been cited as a great place to live by numerous studies and magazine reviews.

The recent upsurge in violence and killings in North Omaha is a direct result of poverty, despair, hopelessness, and a subculture of crime and violence that could care less about well-meaning marches, verbalizations, and, for that matter, prayer. Statements by leaders and politicians are nice but have little to no impact on this culture. Nonprofit efforts have some impact but very small.

Lip service by the leaders of the public and private sectors rings hollow to my ears. My beloved North Omaha needs jobs, contracts, and business outlets for those providing goods and services. Not lip service.

One segment of this maze of overlooked and neglected for-profit companies is the North Omaha Construction Contractors. Well, these contractors say, "Enough is enough."

Recent developments in North Omaha include the Walmart store on Ames, the Learning Community Building on 24th and Seward, and the whopping $2.3 billion CSO [sewer project]. All in North Omaha, all right in the heart of a poverty-stricken area. All with the prospect of having a positive effect on the families of the business owners from North O and subsequently poverty and therefore violence. These projects offered tremendous opportunity for the leaders of the public and private sectors to go beyond lip service and see the positive effect of sharing the wealth. But no contracts to Black contractors were forthcoming.

Now we look ahead: $4.7 million going to be spent at Omaha Public Schools on building and improvements; multi-million-dollar development at the 75 North project; and twenty more years and billions on the CSO project (to name a few). Many, many more are on the drawing board for North Omaha. Will this be more of the same?

The city of Omaha has been giving lip service to the use of North Omaha and South Omaha [a highly Latino and ethnic community] contractors as it relates to the CSO. Also giving lip service to the woes of violence. Attempts to develop a workable plan for involvement by Councilman Gray have been foiled by this administration, and the city canceled the contract of the one African-American business that has made progress in this arena. Canceling the contract of a firm that has attempted and offered a plan, then replacing his contract with lip service.

Enough is enough.

Contractors are investigating methods to stop the CSO [sewer] progress, including civil disobedience and legal remedies directed at the federal and city levels.

This media alert represents the last attempt to challenge the mayor and others to sit down and discuss a plan for involvement. We are not looking for meetings without meaning. The contractors have asked Preston Love Jr. to represent their interests to begin or not to begin a meaningful initiation of a plan for the involvement of businesses from impoverished North Omaha.

Now let us return to the historical development.

PRIMARY 2014: THE GOOD, THE BAD, AND THE UGLY

Most all my writings, including those in this book, were written for the *Omaha Star* newspaper, the only Black weekly newspaper in Nebraska. I write in the *Star* to communicate to my North Omaha Community. The *Star* quotes a circulation of about 10,000 and includes a national audience of former Omaha residents. The articles combine commentary and news stories. Additionally, my articles are widely distributed via email to hundreds within and outside of my community. Some of the articles get picked up by rural newspapers. My focus is an attempt to mobilize thought and actions within my community. Following the 2014 primary election, I wrote this message:

The 2014 primary election is behind us now. Not a pleasant performance by North Omaha given all that was and is at stake. We are a community that is on the mend, with new vitality and many new solutions in progress including the impetus of economic development, which is beginning to pay dividends in jobs and the retention of cash within the community.

That said, our community still has many, many challenges, problems, and needs coupled with our new opportunities. Jobs and job development, educational solutions, health and health care, and crime and violence remain big challenges for our beloved North Omaha. While very few of us dispute those truths, it appears that too many of us seem to be misinformed or uninformed that politics and elected officials can either hurt or help our interest. Why else would our community vote at less than 10 percent in an election determining so many important county and state offices and choices for United States Senate, United States Congress, and Nebraska Governor.

Yes, North Omaha, you voted at a rate in the primary at less than 10 percent. That's ugly.

North Omaha—didn't you see that Dave Domina, the Democrat US Senate candidate, would be running for you and his opponent would be a Tea Party representative in Nebraska? That Democrat Chuck Hassebrook, candidate for Nebraska governor, would be running against

"Wall Street Pete" Ricketts? That Brad Ashford, the Democrat candidate for US Congress, is running against Lee Terry?

That's bad.

What's good? Our community has another chance to come out and vote for our own self-interest, to show our voting strength, and to recognize that who we vote for will affect our community and our future. Don't get caught up in the unthinking discussion that your vote doesn't make a difference. Are you kidding me?

Vote and get involved to assist the effort to get out to vote, make some calls, knock on some doors, do some data entry, help in a campaign office, pass this book along. Let's get busy.

WHO IS GOING TO
FILL THE VOID?

In a follow-up article, I wrote this:

Yes, there were victories. The voters, North Omahans, and a large amount of Republican voters said enough is enough to Republican Congressman Lee Terry with the result that Democrat Brad Ashford will represent our congressional district. It should be noted that nearly 20,000 Republicans who voted in Douglas County decided not to cast a vote for Lee Terry. Meaning no disrespect, to Mr. Ashford, the Republicans defeated Lee Terry, not us.

The presence of the minimum wage "tide" on the ballot was significant but not enough to lift any boats off the bottom. Hurray for the passage of the meager increase of the minimum wage from $7.25 to $9.00 per hour. A great victory for our community, which has a great number making the minimum wage.

Senate candidate Dave Domina, Governor candidate Chuck Hassebrook, and a slew of

Democratic candidates were drowned by the Republican red tsunami that hit the entire country including our state and, to a large degree, Douglas County.

In my humble opinion, our community has lost its way. We have lost our true understanding of the value and power of the vote, and we have created a disconnect, a void if you will, between the needs of our community and the methodology to fulfill the needs.

We have a large number of nonprofits who are doing a superb job of addressing the needs, led by some dedicated and bright people. The need to fund these efforts falls almost entirely on outside groups, foundations, and donors. That dependence on outside funding brings a complete lack of independence by the leaders of these nonprofits because of the dangers of loss of funding or their positions. This is the reality—not a criticism of the leaders.

This phenomenon leaves a void in leadership in our community. Why else would our community vote in this past election at a mere 30 percent? Why else would our community stand by and let development after development occur in our community without any Black community contractors and very few (if any) Black workers? Why else would we allow many of our great cultural institutions to go underfunded while outside groups come in with lots of money and develop in our community, diluting our culture. I could go on and on. For example, the Malcolm X Foundation, Love Jazz and Arts Center, and the Great Plains Black History Museum suffer financially while the White-based Hope Center and the Bemis thrive. It's happening nationwide in most of the core urban communities from 5 Points in Denver to Harlem in New York.

This community needs capital from within, from us. That will never happen until we demand participation in the developments going on all around us. Demand Economic Inclusion. We need to put our foot down. An example is the $2 billion of development, the CSO project, which is disrupting the flow, jeopardizing our small businesses, and increasing monthly utility bills and yet creating no real business opportunities and very little work for the community it is killing. If we are given opportunity, we will create wealth within the community and free up our leadership to stand up against our plight.

There is a void. Who is going to fill it?

I am vowing to speak out and take leadership in an attempt to build some wealth among our present and new businesses. Please take leadership in your own circles and vow not to let the voids be filled by those outside our community as the election has shown so dramatically.

* * *

Can something be done to mobilize voters? Yes, I am happy to report. The following partnership among North Omaha organizations is a start:

Partnership Formed to Increase Voter Participation in North Omaha

The North Voter Partnership

The NAACP, Interdenominational Ministerial Alliance (IMA), North Omaha Neighborhood Alliance (NONA), and the North Omaha Voter Participation Project have formed a coalition with the mission of increasing voter participation in North Omaha.

Recent turnout (July 2013) in the Omaha municipal election demonstrated the need for such an effort. Turnout in North Omaha in the 2013 mayoral and city council election was a disappointing 13 percent and followed by 23 percent in the general election. Not only were the turnouts dismal, but lack of voters in North Omaha also exposed the 10- to 12-point negative gap between the turnout in the rest of Omaha and that of North Omaha.

This newly formed "Partnership" believes that there is a need for an intensive, comprehensive long-term effort to increase voter participation. That effort will focus on educational development for North Omaha voters, leadership, candidates, and youth. The Partnership will conduct workshops, seminars, forums, and town hall meetings and produce regular communications to the North Omaha community. The effort will also include the development of potential North Omaha candidates and the promotion of North Omahans to run for all available elective offices.

The Partnership has planned these community engagement activities to further the agenda:

- Conduct a survey of North Omaha residents as to their reasons for not voting and seeking input as to what would effect change.

- Host a town hall meeting at the Love Jazz and Art center (24th & Lake).

- Hold town hall meetings at churches and restaurants to meet with the mayor.

Let's look at a similar community—Ferguson, Missouri—and see what difference can be made if Black voters voted.

VOTES COUNT: FERGUSON, MISSOURI

"We are falling into the same trap here in Omaha. Wise up and vote."

Ferguson, Missouri: population 22,000, 67 percent African-American, high poverty, double-digit unemployment, yet the residents have the power to singlehandedly elect the mayor (which includes the appointment of the police chief), the power to singlehandedly elect most of the city council, school board, and other offices.

Yet what do the facts reveal? White mayor, White police chief, five White city council members and just one Black, six members of the school board with just one Black, and fifty-three members of the police force that includes just three Blacks.

Why? Because Blacks in Ferguson voted at 8 percent in the last mayor's race and vote in dismal numbers always. Translation: they have given away their power and now are paying the price. That does not mean that the Whites in charge should get a free ticket to abuse and kill our people, but what it does mean is that we have made it a whole lot easier to abuse and kill our people because we are missing the point.

The point is that they have the ability in Ferguson to control their own destinies mainly by voting. By the way, we are falling into the same trap here in Omaha. Wise up and vote. Do the math. We can improve our situation by voting strong in North Omaha.

Get the point, North Omaha, vote, volunteer, get vocal, but not after some "Ferguson" repeat in our own community. We voted at 8 percent in the primary election (2014) and are chronically underrepresented in leadership and elective positions and suffer from the same poverty and underemployment levels as Ferguson. Sound familiar? Let's determine our own destiny now.

The following position paper on why nonvoters should vote is a sequel to the paper presented at the beginning of this book on the "10 Reasons African-Americans Are Not Engaged in Their Community" which was published in the *Omaha Star*.

Section 2:
The Focus

---

10 REASONS
WHY NONVOTERS
SHOULD VOTE

Your vote matters. Vote.

In the earlier chapter entitled "10 Reasons African-Americans Are Not Engaged in Their Community," the sixth reason given was **failure to connect voting to our lives.**

One of the most frequent comments I hear from a potential voter is this: "My vote does not matter." This is also one of my most difficult arguments, for I often fear that I cannot quickly articulate a short sound bite that would change their minds, because every vote does matter.

As my previous position paper on Ferguson, Missouri, states, Black votes can make a difference in the makeup of the city council, police force, and school board and among high-ranking offices such as mayor. Every vote would count in Ferguson, if the majority of voters (Black voters) would vote.

Their votes [in Ferguson] could have changed the tragic history we see playing out today. In North Omaha and nearly all poor communities, there is a disconnect between voting and our lives. That disconnect is flawed and misguided. Consider the following ten reasons why nonvoters should vote:

1. **Jail time.** Too often members of our community are paraded before a judge based on a committed or accused crime and are found guilty and faced with a sentence. Far too often the sentence does not fit the crime. The judge (and sometimes a jury) decides the time given. Almost all judges are elected and are so-called nonpartisan. In reality their politics, their views on the social issues, are reflected in their sentences (albeit some are mandated). The judges have lots of leeway. These judges are on the ballots. Vote the bad guys with predispositions out and vote fair judges in. Guess what? Your jail time will be more fair and so will your release methodology. Many politicians are backing off the "good time" programs. You should vote against them. Vote. By the way, juries are made up of registered voters only. So you may be called to be on a jury where your vote there will truly matter.

2. **Availability of health care and state Medicaid.** I have worked with the Charles Drew Health Center as a certified counselor assisting the community in the enrollment process under the Affordable Care Act (ACA), called Obamacare by some. Reminder, North Omaha is a community of severe poverty. The design of ACA was to provide health care options to all citizens. Those who were between 100 percent to 500 percent of the national poverty level would receive tax subsidies to offset premium costs. In a high-poverty-laden community many are below the 100 percent level and thus incapable of paying any premium and so do not qualify for the subsidies. But the design provided a safety net at the state level, an expanded Medicaid system that would insure most below the 100 percent level and provide federal dollars to the state to do so. Our state (Nebraska) under our elected governor chose to reject this option thus leaving a great number of our community without a health insurance option. We needed to vote against such politics because the new governor is also rejecting the expansion.

3. **Federal, state, and local financial assistance to the disabled and poor.** In our community, among others, our people need and, after meeting the qualifications, receive financial benefits such as "food stamps," as well as direct benefits to children including nutritional oversight and guidance. These benefits touch housing, food, mental health, and so many more real needs. All of these benefits have become political "soccer" balls being kicked around and are subject to elimination, reduction, or unraveling. Your benefits are not guaranteed and can be taken away at any time. The people with the power to reduce or eliminate your benefits are all elected. You should vote against those who want to limit or eliminate your benefits.

4. **Fair running of elections.** Nebraska law dictates that the sitting governor appoint the Douglas County Election Commissioner to run our elections. Additionally, the job of Deputy Commissioner is appointed by the commissioner (after receiving recommendations from the political party that is the opposite of the governor's party and the party of his commissioner appointee). In other words, a Republican governor will

appoint a Republican commissioner and then the commissioner must appoint a Democrat deputy. Said simply, this is a very political scenario and subject to serious political shenanigans. In the 2008 presidential election, North Omaha played a pivotal role. Great voter turnout, leadership, and a significant voter role resulted in the historic split electoral vote. This role was met with a list of political shenanigans in the 2012 primary. For example, the Republican-led Election Commission summarily closed twelve polling places without consultation or warning, causing pure mayhem for the North Omaha voting public. Many North Omahans believe this move was an attempt to suppress the important North Omaha vote of 2008. My message here is that you have the power with your vote to affect who is elected governor and thus affect who becomes the Election Commissioner, running our elections.

5. **The makeup and accountability of the police force.** You elect a favorable mayor, you will get a more favorable police force and the management of the police force. There are always going to be problems with rogue police officers. The tone and performance of

most of the force is set from the mayor down. Re-read the Ferguson, Missouri, scenario. The fault of Ferguson lies at the hands of the nonvoters of Ferguson. We need to take control of our own destinies. Not voting is wasting our power and giving it away. Take back control. Your vote matters.

6. **The level of your wages (minimum wage).** In the 2014 midterm election, the minimum wage was voted on by the public and it passed, raising the minimum wage in Nebraska from the current federal minimum of $7.25 to $9.00 over the next two years. I do acknowledge that communities and people all over Nebraska needed the increase in order to survive, but no community in Nebraska needed the increase greater than North Omaha. Why then did less than 30 percent of the North Omaha voters even go to the polls? Disconnect, an incredible disconnect that separates the electorate from the reality that we can make a difference, yet these nonvoters don't seem to know it. We got lucky it passed even though we didn't do our part to help ourselves. We must wake up and handle our business.

7. **Elected officials who watch your back and help fight your battles.** Our community needs elected officials who watch your back and help fight your battles. They are elected. Vote them in and keep them if they do. Vote them out if they don't—it's that simple. To not vote then complain about the results? Out of order and grandstanding. A no vote is a double vote to the enemy. We have many battles to fight as a community, and we need all the help we can get.

8. **High-level quality and funding of your kids' education.** It's the school board, stupid. They are voted in. Your vote matters, vote.

9. **Public sector** (city, county, and state governments) **sharing the wealth with our community's business owners.** If we are going to fight for Economic Inclusion we need some "weapons" in our arsenal. The biggest weapon we have against the public sector is the power to defeat the elected officials who control the economic purse strings by voting. You don't vote and they don't share. Your vote matters. Vote.

10. **Our ancestors fought for and died for the right to vote.** Don't disrespect your own legacy. Vote.

Now what?

Well, each of us who is concerned about these facts needs to review this list carefully and go about the business of convincing our families, friends, associates, and others to get wise and start voting.

SELMA: TEACHING HISTORY AND A CIVIC LESSON

Part of the 700 youth who were hosted with free seats, popcorn and a civic lesson at a special showing of the movie Selma

One of our challenges to get our community voting is education. People don't know who to vote for. They don't know who the candidates are or what they stand for or how their votes might affect the Black community. And, sadly, some people are simply not able to vote because of illiteracy or ignorance or fear.

I am pleased to tell you about an initiative among our youth that met with overwhelming success. Here is how I described the event in a press statement:

"What a great day for our youth," stated Pastor T. Michael Williams of Risen Son Baptist Church and President of the Interdenominational Ministerial Alliance (IMA).

The IMA along with the League of Women Voters of Greater Omaha (LWV) partnered with the North Omaha Voter Participation Project and organized this special event at Aksarben Cinema showing the movie *Selma*, January 19 [2015]. The partners were able to raise the money to provide free seats and popcorn for nearly 700 enthusiastic youth from over forty-five youth groups, churches, and mentoring organizations.

Many special guests attended including county assessor Diane Batiatto, newly elected congressman Brad Ashford, OPS board member Yolanda Williams, pastors Backus (Salem Baptist), Ken Allen (Zion Baptist), and Portia Cavitt (Clair United Methodist). Over 300 youths requested but were not able to come because of lack of available seats.

After the movie, the young men and women (aged from 12 to 19) participated in a panel discussion led by Channel 42 journalist Franque Thompson. The panel was made up of Jamie Cooper, President of the Young Professionals Organization; Khris Bridges, UNL student and former North High student; Preston Love Jr., founder of the Voter Project; Pastor T. Michael Williams, UNO Black Studies Instructor; and Peggy Adair, President of the LWV.

The students asked some very insightful questions. They were urged to register, vote and to remind their families to do the same. Because of the tremendous response, the youth attended three different theaters showing *Selma* within the complex.

Sponsors included Omaha Economic Development Corporation, Congressman Brad Ashford, and The Sherwood Foundation, Davis Companies, Urban League, American Harvest, and a host of many other individual donors. The Aksarben Cinema was a gracious host and should be supported by our community in the future.

There is a need for increased civic education. Education on the functions of the branches of government at the local, county, state, and federal level needs to be increased. Elementary, middle school, and high school students should have stronger civic-related education. This will increase voter participation at all levels related to voting: voter self-education, voter registration, volunteering, and voting. So many don't know who or what is on the ballot and what's at stake. A more informed community will vote. Speakers are available from the sponsoring organizations to come to schools and groups to discuss the civic and history lessons.

Once again the Nebraska state legislature will try to enact voter ID laws in Nebraska. Please join our fight against this fourth attempt.

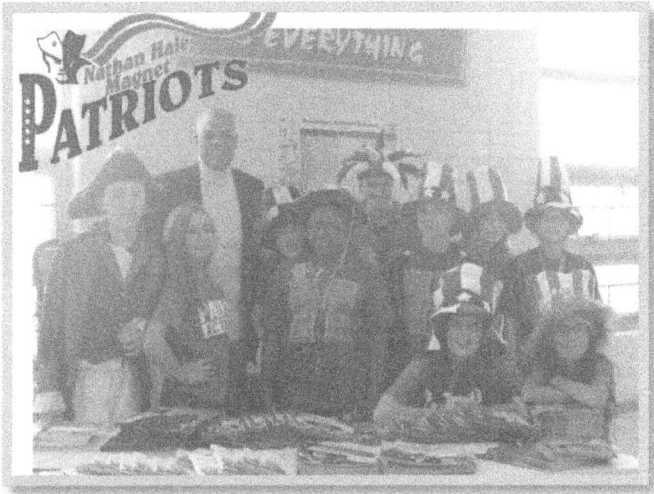

With students from Nathan Hale Middle School.
It was a great civic education event

COMMUNITY ALERT!

VOTER ID LIFTS ITS UGLY HEAD AGAIN IN THE NEBRASKA LEGISLATURE

Two new bills (LB 111 and LB 121) have been introduced in the Nebraska Unicameral to institute voter ID in the state. At least twice before, the activism of many, including a major effort from North Omaha that included renting and filling a busload to Lincoln to lobby and educate the senators against passage, we were successful.

What is voter ID? Voter ID is the title given to attempts to suppress voters. Under any Voter ID law, each voter would be required to obtain state issued identification. Driver's license or a so-called state-issued identification card. The cost averages around $25.00.

Every move requires an updated ID.

Just as the US Senate continues to raise challenges to the Affordable Care Act (forty times by last count), the Nebraska senate refuses to quit on this attempt to undermine and reduce the vote of African-American and Latino voters who will be severely negatively affected.

After the recent showing of the movie *Selma*, voters were reminded of the attempts in the 1960s to stop our vote. Well, here we go again. The ugly head of poll tax is the key to this bill. It costs money for us to get ID, and the enemy knows we have a poor community that cannot afford to spend money for an ID just to vote. *Selma* all over again. I, and many others, will testify against the two bills in Lincoln. But we need the community to rise up against the bill again.

THE NEGATIVE IMPACTS OF VOTER ID - LB III

By Bri McLarty, Director of Voting Rights, bri.mclarty@nereform.org

1. **LB 111 has the potential to disenfranchise over 150,000 Nebraskans.** Nationally 11 percent of all Americans do not have a government-issued photo ID. In Nebraska an estimated 200,000 Nebraskans lack a Nebraska driver's license. Under LB 111, these individuals will have to pay $26.50 for a state ID to receive a ballot.

2. **Restrictive voter ID laws impact and disenfranchise minority voters.** Other states have found photo ID requirements to disproportionately impact minority populations.

3. **The current address requirement in LB 111 disenfranchises low-income and young voters.** LB 111's current address requirement is a hindrance to high mobility populations, requiring those voters to pay $26.50 for a new ID to exercise their constitutional right to vote.

4. **LB 111 would charge students a poll tax to vote in Nebraska.** Students who register to vote at their school address would be required to pay $26.50 to change their valid driver's license in order to receive a ballot.

5. **LB 111 would make it harder for senior citizens to receive a ballot.** For those senior citizens no longer driving, LB 111 would require them to pay $26.50 to obtain a state ID solely for the purpose of voting.

6. **County budgets will bear the cost of LB 111.** In 2013 the DMV determined 65,574 Nebraska driver's license holders did not have their current residence on their license. Under LB 111 these individuals would have to fill out a provisional ballot, costing the county $33 per ballot, over $2.16 million statewide.

7. **Providing free driver's licenses to voters could cost Nebraska over $9 million annually.**

8. **LB 111 "indigent voter" is not defined and does not eliminate the burden on the vast majority of Nebraska voters.**

9. **Voting is a constitutional right given the highest protection possible in Nebraska.** The Nebraska Constitution states Nebraskans shall have the right to vote free of hindrance or impediment, and LB 111's photo ID requirement places an undue burden on voters.

10. **Voter fraud is not an issue in Nebraska.** Deputy Secretary of State Neil Erickson has testified before the Government, Military and Veterans Affairs committee that Nebraska does not experience any voter fraud in Nebraska.

I testified on January 23, 2015, on LB 111 and LB 121 before the Nebraska Legislature. Here is the text of my statement:

Good afternoon.

My name is Preston Love Jr., Senatorial District 11 in Omaha. I will be seventy-three this year, and I live in my beloved North Omaha. Born and raised in North Omaha, I attended public schools in the '50s and graduated from the University of Nebraska here in Lincoln with a BS in economics in 1966.

I had the honor to letter in track and football while at NU playing in the Orange and Cotton Bowls for Bob Devaney. Please note that in the '60s I was living in the vacuum of growing up, playing sports, and was not directly involved in the civil rights movement. That vacuum, however, never isolated me from bigotry and racism, including some while playing for the Big Red.

I worked for IBM for nearly twelve years and retired a junior executive. In the mid-1960s, Blacks in the management structure were rare in corporate America and IBM. I retired from IBM and moved to Atlanta. After an unsuccessful business venture by the early 1980s, I had become fully embedded into the tight-knit civil rights community in Atlanta.

Under then-Mayor Andrew Young, I served as Commissioner of Planning among other positions as appointed. As I stated, I became an insider in the complex world of the civil rights community based in Atlanta and as such became the Deputy Campaign Manager for Presidential Candidate Jesse Jackson in 1984. I went on to become a national political resource within the Black communities around the USA. I have been active politically for over thirty years and will become an Adjunct Professor for the University of Nebraska–Omaha this fall teaching Black Politics in the Black Studies Department.

There is a point here! (Besides my bio.) My unique experiences have left me with unparalleled historic experiences, wisdom as well as some academic research that that can contribute to this discussion.

This past Monday, January 19, I, along with several other great organizations, organized a wonderful event. We raised the money and offered to over forty-five youth groups and churches, free seats and popcorn to over 700 youth and a handful of adults to see the historic movie *Selma*. And we provided them an after-movie panel discussion on civic and history lessons therein. I also sat on that panel.

I have had a personal relationship with almost every significant figure portrayed in that movie and as such have heard their story and backstories surrounding the history depicted in the movie. The pain and history were told to me by the likes of Congressman John Lewis, Former UN ambassador and Atlanta Mayor Andrew Young, and many more.

What do we know?

We know that during the mid-'60s, many, many people were beaten, maimed, and killed (Black and White) in order to simply get the right to vote.

We know that the violence was only one of the many impediments created to bar Negros from voting: gerrymandering, grandfather clauses, literacy tests, required property ownership, extreme inconveniences such as county registrar open to Negroes at short and unpredictable hours, voter rolls purging, and poll taxes to state a few.

What do I know?

I know the reasons. Notwithstanding pure racism of the times, the core reason those impediments were imposed on Negroes was because those Black human beings had the numbers to vote anybody in and anybody out. Plain and simple. Mr. Jim Crow was not going to allow that.

I know that in 2008 my community voted heavily for Barack Obama. And after analysis it was easy to identify those strong Obama precincts in North Omaha (and South Omaha, for that matter).

Well, in the 2012 primary season, low and behold our election commissioner closed half of the precincts in North Omaha. Confusion was rampant among our voters. Seniors, poor, and handicapped voters living in Omaha Housing Authority's high rises (and who voted heavily for Obama) needed only to come down to the lobby to vote. But their polling places were moved to another location, forcing them to leave a building with a polling place to vote. And voters from outside the building were directed to vote in the high rise.

Additionally, distances to polling places were impossible for many. The highest voting precinct in North Omaha for Obama was sent letters (approximately 1,300 voters) to go vote at a polling place that was in fact closed, creating not only confusion but mistrust that still lingers today.

What I know is that these ugly scenarios are reminders that the scenes in the movie *Selma* are slowly turning into a new reality in 2015, all over this country. Hopefully not in Nebraska.

Voter ID has been found around the country to disproportionately affect poor and minorities and the rural communities. The 1965 Voting

Rights Act is slowly being dismantled. The Nebraska voting system is *not* broken, there is no fraud, what are we fixing with Voter ID? I was taught in long ago if it's not broke don't fix it.

Don't put Nebraska on the list of states trying to hinder voting!

Thank you.

The Economics of the CSO Project Disenfranchisement

The Economics of the CSO Project Disenfranchisement has residuals: Hopelessness, crime, violence, and reduced tax contribution. North Omaha is a community of vast disenfranchised poverty. If you reduce poverty in North Omaha, you will increase the hopes of many, reduce crime and violence, reduce the costs related to policing the community, and increase the flow of taxes among many other positive effects to North Omaha stakeholders.

For over two decades now, deep storage tunnels, and what the tunneling industry calls combined sewer overflow (CSO) interceptor systems have formed the backbone of an industry with projects that many of the largest cities in America and sewer districts have been obliged to adopt as part of a nationwide program to reduce overflows of foul and polluted water into the rivers, creeks, and harbors of the nation.

Since the 1990s, a total of 772 cities and districts have been identified by the Federal Environmental Protection Agency (EPA) as needing urgent action to tackle problems associated with operating outdated combined sewer overflow (CSO) systems incapable of dealing with modern demand requirements. Omaha, Nebraska, is one of those cities.

This project offers a unique and significant opportunity to be inclusive and create a sustainable middle class founded on business ownership (and the employees of these businesses) in the poverty-stricken area of North Omaha.

The project can provide construction employment work for an industry and a few high-profile construction companies. A number of high-profile tunnels designed in the 1990s and 2000s are now under construction in Indianapolis (Deep Rock Connector Tunnel in 2012), Washington, D.C. (first launched on 4.5-mile Blue Plains Tunnel in July 2013), North East Ohio (Cleveland Euclid Creek Tunnel in 2012), and Columbus (2011 Tunnel).

The much-lauded and ongoing TARP deep tunnel system for Chicago is an early blueprint. CSO tunnels have also been completed in Seattle for King County (2005, $165 million), Portland (2005 to 2010, $650 million), and a long program of construction of all large-scale deep storage and CSO tunnel projects that are either completed, in construction, or cost estimated since 1998, is in the region of $4 billion.

Within the industry as well as municipalities, there is wavering on the construction time commitment as well as expense of these projects. For example, the DC Water Authority is one of several water authorities looking at green infrastructure as a natural way to manage stormwater by absorbing rain before it enters the sewer or stormwater system. DC Water awarded $1 million in prize money to seven local design teams at its specially convened Green Infrastructure Summit.

This technology phase shift is viewed as an opportunity. In spite of these potential phase shifts, the investment amounts are significant, the need is clear. The development commitment remains clear in the face of the move to green technologies. What is consistently especially here in Omaha is the need for the increased involvement of the Omaha small business community in both the technology change, as well as the implementation.

The language of the Long Term Control Plan (LTCP) states: "To foster an understanding of the CSO Program within minority and emerging community groups and develop a collaborative relationship with neighborhoods."

"It will be necessary to make sure that the public is aware of how its fees are being spent, the benefits of the Program, details on the ratepayer assistance program, local job creation, and what construction impacts will occur and when..."

These words, issued in potentially 772 city projects, cannot be allowed to ring hollow in the face of an ever-widening economic divide, and here in Omaha, the outright destruction of established, working solutions to train, certify, and ensure the success of local minority construction businesses. This destruction took place without thought for an alternative working solution. This malicious intent cannot be tolerated.

With that said, the **Nebraska Democratic Party supports efforts by North Omaha contractors, neighborhood associations, clergy, and other stakeholders challenging the City of Omaha to clearly define a working solution for North Omaha contractor**

inclusion, associated with the $3.2 billion CSO Project. Without this program, the city has clearly defined its plan to ignore North Omaha contractors and businesses, and in turn destroy a viable mechanism for business ownership, local business growth, wage growth, and sustainable economic growth for this local community.

LET'S KEEP THE FOCUS ON CSO AND WHAT'S AT STAKE:
GROWTH OF WEALTH, REDUCTION OF POVERTY IN NORTH OMAHA

Below is a press briefing given to the media:

Thank you for coming. I am sitting with several representatives, key stakeholders, in their quest to improve our beloved North Omaha. Clergy, neighborhood associations, leadership of the United Minority Contractors, and others.

My purpose today is to keep the focus on CSO and what's at stake: the growth of wealth and reduction of poverty in North Omaha.

Quickly, we have gone to "Preston Love Jr. against the mayor [Jean Stothert]." Unfortunate and untrue. It is "Preston Love Jr. against poverty within his community." Whatever it is, let's keep the focus on what's at stake.

First, besides some less-than-serious comments about indirect solutions, the mayor's major response to our comments at the press conference last week was that she had a draft plan. Let me summarize my problem with the so-called plan.

1. It was entitled "Diversity Action Organization." Our challenge never dealt with diversity. It deals with poverty and the quadrant of the city that needs an economic stimulus. Not minority stimulus if that is the diversity reference. Diversity will take care of itself if we get economic stimulus. By the way, the mayor's plan fails any test of diversity.

2. The mayor's plan had little if any vetting with the stakeholders, in spite of many "town hall" meetings and/or other outreach. That step was overlooked and was needed.

3. The mayor's "plan" is a compilation of thoughts, an organization chart, and in my humble evaluation lacks the clarity for implementation and includes targets, tracking, accountability, and frankly some oddities. Example: The box labeled Collaborative Partners. Under the box is "other programs" and "management." What does that mean to the reader?

4. I could go on and on. I won't.

The mayor's plan: It is my understanding that there is a supporting document with more specifics, an "Action Plan." If that is the case, I am encouraged and supportive of the idea of some real specifics. The one-sheet "plan" is water under the bridge, and I am excited about a possible action scenario.

There has been available to the mayor via Councilman Gray an alternate plan titled "Creating a Strong Urban Based Contracting Class in Omaha." We highly endorse that plan, highly. It was created by a diverse collaborative of experts including HDR and Dick Davis, a nationally recognized expert and an very successful Omaha-based business owner. Davis has a track record of providing project and contractor support services.

He has a successful and stellar record with the city doing just that and yet his contract was not renewed by the mayor. By the way, the cost of his contract was essentially paid for by savings to the city that were obtained from bid reductions. We want his kind of expertise and his knowledge of the North Omaha contractors fully involved in the implementation of any "Action Plan" of the mayor.

It is my understanding that a new contract with Mr. Davis is being evaluated. He is an expert and his diversity is not relevant. As a positive move forward, we urge the adoption of his contract, but more importantly his precise methodology to achieve what I am challenging the city about. Moving forward with his involvement would be a great sign of progress and take us from the perceived "Preston Love Jr. versus the mayor" and a move us to "What's at Stake: Growth of Wealth, Reduction of Poverty in North Omaha."

We want to commend the city council Democrats and Republicans for their beginning involvement in this matter, to ensure that this city addresses this source of poverty and reaps the residual benefits down the road. It is my understanding that the legislative branch is weighing in on positive and focused solutions and inclusions for North Omaha. Thank you. We stand ready to address the council if invited and to assist in any way to further their effort.

Lastly, I am encouraged that process is being and can be made. But the stakes are too high and time is of the essence. We would urge the city to see this as we see it, as an urgent dilemma.

Attorney Dave Domina, one of our nation's top attorneys, has agreed to represent a litigation challenge to the current state of affairs relating to the exclusions of CSO, if asked. I hope we don't have to go there.

CONTRACTORS CHALLENGE MAYOR TO SHARE THE WEALTH

WITH NORTH OMAHA CONTRACTORS AND OTHER BUSINESSES

On Monday, February 9, in a press conference held at OIC (Omaha Opportunities Industrialization Center), over forty-five contractors, neighborhood association leaders, business owners and clergy delivered a message to the mayor: "Enough is enough."

Too much work is being done and planned and not enough sharing of the wealth with our businesses.

Here is the statement read by Preston Love Jr. who said, "As of this moment we are putting our foot down, and one way or another the sharing will happen or there will be work stoppage." After the press conference Love said the ball is in the mayor's court. If there is no positive movement, litigation will be forthcoming.

The Statement: North Omaha Contractors say, "Enough is enough."

Breaking News: North Omaha is a poverty-stricken community. A community surrounded by vast wealth, booming economy, unemployment under 5 percent, aggressive economic growth, and construction.

Breaking News: Where you have poverty you have exponential crime, sociopathic subcultures, and violence.

Omaha has been cited as a great place to live by numerous studies and magazine reviews.

Recent upsurge in violence and killings in north Omaha is a direct result of poverty, despair, hopelessness, and a subculture of crime and violence that could care less about well-meaning marches, verbalizations, and, for that matter, prayer. Statements by leaders and politicians are nice but have little to no impact on this culture. Nonprofit efforts have some impact but very small.

Lip service by the leaders of the public and private sectors rings hollow to my ears. My beloved North Omaha needs jobs, contracts, and business outlets for those providing goods and services. Not lip service.

One segment of this maze of overlooked and neglected for profit companies are the North Omaha Construction Contractors. Well these contractors say, "Enough is enough."

This statement goes on, but is repeated in its entirety previously.

An additional release of my testimony before the Omaha City Council:

For Immediate Release 3/30/2015

Preston Love Jr.

North Omaha Stakeholders Support the Initiative to Create Allowances for Contractors Committed to Hiring, Training, and Retaining Employees.

I speak as a native of my beloved community, North Omaha. I speak for many north Omaha contractors and contractor laborers, the North Omaha based United Minority Contractors Association, numerous Neighborhood Associations and supported by many of our North Omaha Clergy. Though I am a community advocate I do not claim to represent 100% of my community—who does?

What I can assure is, however, that there is no disagreement about the realities facing our community. Vast poverty and the residuals of poverty; hopelessness, crime, violence and reduced tax contribution. You reduce poverty in North Omaha, you will increase the hopes

of many. Reduce crime and violence, reduce
the cost related to policing the community and
increase the flow of taxes among many other
positive effects to North Omaha and the city
overall. The "finding" section (section 10-331) of
this ordinance states it well. This city has been
nearly blind, from economic cataracts, if you
will, blind to economic inclusion.

The solution is simple but underutilized.
Provide jobs, business opportunities and
contracts to our North Omaha contractors
(Black and White). Those wages and revenues
to our residents will have dynamic and positive
ripple effects as those dollars circulate in
the community.

Sooner or later leadership in the greater
Omaha community and the city government will
realize the positive overall social and economic
impact of dealing with solutions to poverty in
the northeast quadrant of this city.

So where are we?

This ordinance will go a long way to improve
one cataract: jobs. We applaud this positive
movement and leadership of the city council.
This is a needed ordinance and only one

solution, but it is an initiative directed toward jobs. Jobs for a poor and challenged community. Is this solution perfect? No, but a positive step toward that will impact poverty by stimulating jobs. We highly support the initiative and hope each of you will support it too.

In contrast, we have challenged the Executive Branch to address contractors, the other cataract. Providing work and inclusion of North Omaha contractors in the $2.3 billion CSO project is critical. Most of this work is being done in our backyards. I don't think this city is ready to step up to the discussion of all the work being done citywide. But we are challenging the Executive Branch to set policy and put in place a plan for implementation, performance measures coupled with goals, program tracking and accountability. Get the other cataract removed, address the lack of economic inclusion for the North and South Omaha contractors and we can have a clear vision for a new city of Omaha. One that is addressing all of its residents.

I respectfully request that the city council ensure that any plan submitted by the Executive Branch regarding the contractors, be fully vetted with the aforementioned components and with the stakeholders from our community. Key personnel slated to implement any plan should be seasoned and experienced in this arena (not just good and smart people who may not have the heart or any clue relating to the inclusion of North and South Omaha and small and emerging contractor businesses.

In addition to this ordinance dealing will jobs, we hope your leadership will include serving as a check and balance to the Executive Branch plans and provide a clear vision of the prize at hand: a prosperous city in all sectors.

Thank you.

PRESTON LOVE JR. OFFERS BLACK POLITICS CLASS AT UNO

UNIVERSITY OF NEBRASKA—OMAHA

Starting Fall Semester 2015

COURSE: BLACK POLITICS

COURSE OBJECTIVE

(1) To instruct on the evolution of Black Politics beginning with the passage of the 15th Amendment to the US Constitution and the major historical events affecting Black politics up to and including the current era, (2) To provide a perspective on the major historical and current events that have impacted or are impacting Black Politics, (3) To provide insight into Black Politics during and since the passage of the 1965 Voting Rights Act.

REQUIRED READING:

African American Politics

Kendra King, Edition 1

ISBN: 0745632807

ISBN-13: 9780745632803

Publisher: Wiley (January, 2010)

Economic Cataracts

Preston Love Jr.

ISBN-13: 978-0-9964464-1-9

Publisher: Preston Publishing
(June 23, 2015)

In addition to the text, instructor will provide powerpoint material, relevant papers and articles, and other readings as assigned.

EPILOGUE

The fight continues with the City of Omaha, home of many poverty stricken—and Warren Buffett.

Greater Omaha unemployment is at 2.5 percent, but in North Omaha, it is 22 percent.

We will prevail with the city in 2015. It will continue to be harsh and angry but we will prevail. Meanwhile, opportunities for our minority contractors are popping up all over the city at many of our public and private developments. We certainly take partial credit for completely redefining the dialogue and focusing the entire city on the plight of North Omaha and the need for Economic Inclusion. Seeking to remove the economic cataracts that has grown over so many urban communities.

Work will continue, addressing all elements of the fatal urban community disengagement.

Stay tuned – victory is in sight.

ABOUT THE AUTHOR

Preston Love Jr. is a community and political activist. He worked for key political figures such as Atlanta Mayor Andrew Young and Chicago Mayor Harold Washington. He was campaign manager for The Reverend Jesse Jackson, the first Black man to run for President of the United States.

Preston Love Jr. pursued work in the civil rights movement early in his career and is passionate about continuing his work in his hometown neighborhood of North Omaha. He is presently teaching politics at the University of Nebraska–Omaha.

He graduated with a degree in economics from the University of Nebraska–Lincoln in 1966. He played football for the Big Red and Bob Devaney and played in both the Orange and Cotton Bowls.

What follows is a more detailed profile of Preston Love Jr.

PERSONAL POLITICAL HISTORY

Advisor, computer consultant and city government appointee to Former congressman, UN Ambassador and successful candidate for Mayor of Atlanta: Andrew Young (1980)

Advisor, computer consultant and field organizer to Former congressman, and successful candidate for Mayor of Chicago: Harold Washington (1983)

Advisor, computer consultant and field Manager to the Re-election Campaign of Mayor of Chicago: Harold Washington (1987)

National Campaign Manager, Jesse Jackson for President 1984; August '83–November, 1984

First Executive Director: National Rainbow Coalition

Campaign Manager 1988 and 1990 Mel Reynolds of Congress (CD 2, Chicago, Ill.)

Advisor to or managed over 20 other campaigns from US House to local offices in over 5 cities

1990: Led a major effort and increased historic low registration and turnout in North Omaha under the theme

"Register your vote not your frustrations" Effort was a significant acknowledged factor for the election of Ben Nelson for Governor

Founder, organizer and leader of the North Omaha Voter Participation Project.

- Organized a working coalition with political, social, civic, community and church groups every election since return to Omaha in 2006."

- Voter registration and turnout in North Omaha and have beaten the historic averages.

NORTH OMAHA
POLITICAL HISTORY

Highlights of the North Omaha Political successes under the leadership of Preston Love Jr. include 2 awards in 2008(AK Sorority and Douglas county Dems); Campaign Manager for Candidate Ben Gray for Omaha City Council; led the North Omaha effort to stop the Recall effort against Mayor Suttle (South Omaha did maintain significant support, North Omaha was trending to not maintain, Ben Gray and the tireless work of the Voter Project members and countless volunteers under Preston's leadership, North Omaha held and the recall failed.(2010)"

2008 Credited with the key leadership in the historic split vote (Electoral Vote) in the 2008 Nebraska Congressional District 2 Presidential Election

2012 North Omaha leader and central figure in all voter initiatives. Leader of community efforts to fight recent attempts to suppress Black, poor and Latino votes, see attachment for summary of challenges and activities

2012 Field Organizer, Columbus, Ohio, for Organizing for America (Obama)

2013 Campaign Field Director—Ben Gray Re-Election successful Campaign

2013 Interdenominational Ministerial Alliance Award winner (Drum Major Award for Accountability) for work for North Omaha 2012 Election

2014 Dave Domina for the US Senate: Deputy Campaign Manager

2015 Adjunct Professor, University of Nebraska—Omaha, Black Studies Department

OTHER RECENT ACTIVITIES

Founder: North Omaha 1st Monday Forum; Monthly lunch and public forum with speaker discussing full range of issues/program affecting our community; attended by approx. 50-60 people monthly (2013)

Founder: Hungry Club; Monthly lunch and public forum with speaker discussing full range of issues/program affecting our community; attended by approx. 50-60 people monthly (2007)

Candidate for the Metropolitan Utilities District Board of Directors (unsuccessful: received 43,000 Votes)

Community Advocate and Activist

Regular Guest Lecturer on politics and voting rights at UNO and Metro Community College

North Omaha Voter Participation Project: Founder/Organizer/Leader 2006

Researcher, writer and one man show Chautauqua & Performer: "Adam Clayton Powell"

Researcher, writer and one man show & performer: Preston Love Jr., "From Cotton Bowl to Cotton Candy"

George W. Norris Lecture: Keynote Address by Preston Love Jr. University of Nebraska— Kearney (2009)

Awards, Affiliations and Distinctions

AKA Sorority for Community Service (2009);

Douglas County Democratic Party: Chairman's Award (2009);

2013 Interdenominational Ministerial Alliance (IMA) Award winner (Drum Major Award for Accountability) for work for North Omaha 2012 Election

Graduate of LEADERSHIP ATLANTA

Actively serving the following organizations

Literacy Center of the Midlands; Board Member-former

Tech High Auditorium Steering Committee

NE Omaha Weed and Seed Steering Committee-former

Voter Participation subcommittee: Empower-
ment Network

Board Member: United Urban Voters League

Volunteer Fundraiser/Marketing John Beasley
Theater

Advisory Committee: Catholic Charities, St.
Martin De Porres

Active Member Antioch Church of God
in Christ. President of the men's
department

Community Liaison to Nebraska First Church of
God in Christ Jurisdictional Prelate John
O. Ford

Key Formal Non-Political Employment History

Charles Drew Health Center, *Certified Application Counselor (Affordable Care Act), 2013*

North Omaha Contractors Alliance; *Executive Director,* 2009 to 2011

American Harvest Company; *Analyst and Consultant,* September 2006–September 2008

The Preston Group; *Owner, Small Business Consultant,* July 1990–September 1995

City of Atlanta, GA; Andrew Young, Mayor, *Director of the Office of Management Systems and Commissioner of Planning,* January 1981–July 1983

Datamart, Inc. *Founder, President: Atlanta's first Retail Computer Store,* January 1979–June 1981

IBM Data Processing Division, *National Marketing Manager; Manufacturing Industry Marketing;* White Plains, NY, October 1966–November 1978.

ACKNOWLEDGMENTS

To the scores of family, supporters, partners, volunteers and researchers who have been assisting my leadership effort for years. United Minority Contractors (Officers Ron Jefferson and Bishop Larry Helm), Ellen and Willie Paschall, Dr. Herbert Rhodes, Frank Peak, Vicky Parks, sister Portia Love, Diana Upchurch, Myra Butts, researcher Morris Jones, Mike Moroney, Ben Gray, Dick Davis, Ella Willis , Beverly Frazier, the late Orville and Savelia Johnson, Carolyn Thiele, Dave and Carol Domina, Jay Meyers, Tom Osborne, Andrew Young, Rev. Jesse Jackson, Pastor Otis Moss, Pastor T Michael Williams, Bishop L. F. Thuston, D.Th., Nathanal Goldston, Jimmy Hall, Rodney Weed, Ed Martin, Dr. Williard Wright, Eliga Ali, and many more and family Norman, Richie, Beverly, Lora, and Lisa, Bishop John O. Ford, Pastor Larry Taylor, I say God Bless you.

BONUS SUPPLEMENT

State of the State: Economic Inclusion for North Omaha Via Construction Opportunities for our Contractors

Congratulations! North Omaha Economic Inclusion is finally on the table.

Since the beginning of 2015, I, along with many other leaders and stakeholders, have demanded a change in the way construction in North Omaha would be conducted. We demanded that the dialogue be changed from business as usual to how will public institutions initiate Economic Inclusion in their respective millions of dollars of construction in the backyard of our poverty stricken North Omaha.

By in large, you, the North Omaha community, have supported us. Thank you.

Congratulations. We have changed the dialogue. We have changed the way these institutions are approaching their multimillion dollar projects. By this time in 2016, this community will be seeing the influx of capital into our community and the first significant impact on poverty in our lifetime. That's victory, and we should stand tall and affirm our role in it.

Let me summarize where we are in the following pages.

State of the State: Economic Inclusion for North Omaha Via Construction Opportunities for Our Contractors

CHI

$30 million development off 24th & Cuming
Owner: Creighton
Prime Contractor: McCarthy Construction

McCarthy has aggressively sought out North (and South) Omaha and minority contractors. The first of three phases of the development has produced several contracts for minority and North Omaha subcontractors, and plans are underway for that to continue in the upcoming and larger phases. Excellent beginning.

OPS

$421 million bond Issue funding multiple
construction projects (many in North Omaha)
Owner: OPS, $16 million
Consultant: Jacobs
Prime Contractors: Chosen for each separate project

OPS set a 7 percent goal for Inclusion. Jacobs
set a great framework for Inclusion. They set
up a contractor academy which is positive and
ongoing. JE Dunn became the Prime on the first
major project, and because of projected budget
overrun, the time-sensitive project (Ponca Hills
School) must be rebid.

Other key projects have been stalled because of
the failure on the part of the larger contractors to
bid. (Note: for any project to move forward three
bids must be entered. That has been a problem to
date.) Projects that have to be rebid face challenges
for completion within the scheduled time. There
are implications as a result of stalled projects.

1) OPS must scramble to complete these school
projects by the time school starts and contractors
face penalties.

2) Are white contractors reluctant to bid
because they don't like the idea of having to share

the spoils with small, emerging, and minority companies as dictated by OPS/Jacobs?

3) The small, emerging, and minority companies who were anticipating opportunities at OPS this summer have to wait until these stalled projects are straightened out. That delays the OPS victories, but I believe they are coming. Excellent potential, fair beginning.

MCC

$90 million project building four new facilities on the Fort Omaha Campus
Owner: MCC
Prime Contractor: Kiewit

In spite of strong community-based support, the MCC Board voted not to force goals onto Kiewit and the project construction.

For the record, once a Project Owner hires a Prime Contractor, the project implementation flows entirely to the Prime. If the Owner does not impose hard, specific, and enforceable measures and goals to the Prime, the Inclusion will be subject to the Prime doing the right thing.

Kiewit has a checkered record of Inclusion. I have attended all of the meetings to date that Kiewit has had relating to the project.

Additionally, the United Minority Contractors Alliance hosted the Kiewit project leadership in June and are attempting to work with them to provide assistance toward Inclusion.

The MCC Board and Kiewit have verbally indicated a strong desire to be inclusive on this project. My current assessment is that Kiewit will have a difficult time. Kiewit, like many other very large construction firms, has long established paradigms and "ways of doing business," many of which will make it hard to adjust to the culture of small, emerging and minority businesses.

To their credit, they have acknowledged their willingness to break contracts into smaller bites, but that alone won't get us there. My hope is the Kiewit Executive teams will be open to the outreach necessary to receive small, emerging, and minority companies. Without that, the results are going to be minimal. Inclusion on this project will require TLC.

Highlander Project

$90 million development project in and around
30th and Parker
Owner: 75 North Revitalization Corporation
Prime Contractor: Lund-Ross

Lund/Ross is the new kid on the block, having just had their first meeting with small, emerging, and minority companies this past week. My first impressions for Inclusion from this project are very positive and very optimistic. While I have not seen any written external documents, the clearly-articulated policies and specifics for Inclusion are excellent. The key is a very involved and connected owner—in this case, the 75 North Corp. Additionally, there is a unique and added component: the existence of a relationship with a nationally-known developer with an excellent Inclusion track record (i.e. Purpose Built Communities organization out of Atlanta). Goals above 25 percent, revolving contractor cash flow loans, assistance on material procurement, and more provide a great potential for Inclusion.

It should be noted that it appears that the 75 North team, which includes Lund-Ross, recognizes and are prepared to deal with the aforementioned small and emerging and minority company culture that is critical to a functional and successful Inclusion operation.

Excellent potential and we are very optimistic about this project's Inclusion commitment.

City of Omaha CSO

$2 billion city projects, primarily in the N.E. sector of the city (North Omaha)
Owner: City of Omaha
Construction consultant: CH2m Hill
Prime Contractors: Chosen for each separate project

After nearly five months of acrimonious dialogue with the Executive Branch and a show of early leadership by the Legislative Branch, we are finally at a point where I feel confident, as do others, that we have reached a point to declare victory. We are ready now for the contractors to begin to attempt to do significant business with the City and CSO Project. This was the point from the beginning. Our challenge to the city appears to be met with a meaningful effort to be inclusive as it relates to CSO contracts. Additionally, under the leadership of the City Council and with the Mayor, the City has allocated $400,000 toward the development of workers via Workforce Development. That is positive too.

In early June 2015, Councilman Ben Gray stepped up and brought community leadership together resulting in a communication from him, me, Dick Davis and a number of other black elected officials. This served as an olive branch. Because of the positive steps by the City and particular Inclusion steps for CSO, we desired a truce and a meeting to clear the air and fashion ways for working together towards successful Inclusion.

The City Inclusion steps, while positive, are in the infancy stage and will require much nourishing going forward. While the Mayor seemed reluctant to meet with anyone other than Ben Gray, she has now agreed to meet with our delegation in the latter part of June. I want to commend the latest manifestation of Inclusion with the recent announcement of the CSO $90 million project for Saddle Creek Retention Basin and establishing a 4.5 percent SEB goal along with a .5 percent goal for Tier 1.

Until last week, the City had not complied with the City ordinance that requires goal setting at all levels including each contract, not just at the Mayor's office. The step of assigning a goal to the Saddle Creek contract is a major victory for Inclusion. We commend the Mayor on this step. Additionally, the stated intent to assign goals to all future contracts is major and good. There are many additional steps that we would like to recommend, and we will do so this month and as part of future meetings.

It should be noted that we are at the beginning stages where we can impact poverty via contracts with our North Omaha contractors. We still have lots of work to do to maximize success. That's why we wish to meet with the administration.

In summary, we celebrate victory—
Economic Inclusion has begun.

Other Victories

Additionally, there have been some other noteworthy victories:

- We have changed the dialogue for most public institutions, thus putting Economic Inclusion on the table.

- We have galvanized and unified the relationships with most all of our Black elected officials around this issue and going forward on other issues.

- We have drawn a line in the sand for future Economic Inclusion efforts for North Omaha non-contracting businesses, and I expect other initiatives to spring forward

- We have renewed the faith and hopes of our North Omaha contracting base. They are re-energized. Retired and experienced contractors, like Fred Newson and Tommy Adams, are returning to consult and mentor as well as participate.

- We have chipped away at the unfortunate myth about our contractors. We have capable and qualified contractors. Many young people have recently expressed the desire to get in the business.

- We have flushed out a few in our community who are willing to sell out in the midst of a fight for our community survival.

- We have captured the support of so many stakeholders, leadership and others, and that has added to our unity.

- We have captivated and activated an underground network of young professionals and intellectuals that will pay dividends to North Omaha in years to come.

- We affirm the role of the North Omaha clergy in being a steady, spiritual voice to all during the ordeal.

- We have turned on the faucet of economic growth and wealth in our community. While there is now a drip, we see the prospect of a strong stream of growth down the road.

What's Next?

- To ensure success for our contractors after they get contracts, there are sixteen terms and conditions which are the most commonly needed. All of these items must be individually negotiated and mutually agreed upon by both parties before the contract is executed. Failure to recognize these factors has contributed to poorly-performed work under the contract. The terms and conditions fall within these four major summarized categories:

1. Bond and Insurance Requirements
2. Contract Schedules
3. Payment Provisions
4. Contractual Disputes and Penalties

- The Davis Companies provides services and consulting to their CDS participants at no cost. Either the Davis Companies or an equally-qualified company should be utilized for success with our contractors.

- We'll need continued pressure on the leadership and boards of our public institutions to help them understand the value of an economically healthy North Omaha.

- Midway through 2015 we have reached a milestone, but we're not at the end of fighting poverty by any means.

- Removal of or significant changes to the City's licensing requirement. This is a significant hurdle for most small contractors. Until changes are made, there is a need for workshops for the contractors to help them prepare to take the exams. There are also costs involved. We must have conversations now with the Chamber of Commerce to assist us with this.

- There is a need for extensive estimating training and/or help for our contractors.

- Almost all of the public institutions mentioned need to hire an experienced, knowledgeable consultant to manage and oversee their Inclusion implementations.

- We need to provide a meeting clearinghouse to minimize the conflicts arising between institutions as they conduct the numerous meetings to further their respective programs. Currently scheduling conflicts are increasing.

- Mayor's comments in June newspaper articles about Councilman Gray's motives in seeking to be elected as President of the City Council were self-serving. In truth, Gray's request for a meeting with the Mayor was the result of meetings with Preston Love, Jr., Dick Davis and other black elected officials. The email requesting a group meeting stated our objective: to clear the air and fashion ways to work together moving forward.

- The one-on-one with Gray was the Mayor's idea as a condition to meet our group. The Presidency of the Council was not on the group agenda.

- It was a gamble to meet one-on-one with the Mayor, after reading her comments in the *OWH* I feel it was a mistake. Once again this Mayor presents her spin in order to discredit Mr. Gray.

- For me, I withdraw my desire to clear the air because this Mayor doesn't get it. I will continue to work with the all of those who are willing to listen to our community to enhance the recent positive steps made by the Mayor for Inclusion. Meeting with her will not further our cause.

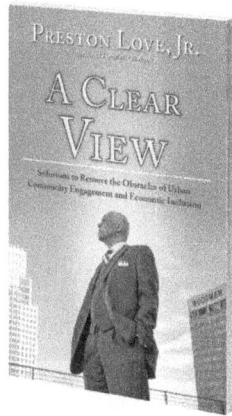

A Clear View: Solutions to Remove the Obstacles of Urban Community Engagement and Economic Inclusion contains a collection of articles by Preston Love, Jr. It includes new thought-provoking material to set a strategic framework for economic development in urban communities, and develops and discusses short-term, tactical solutions for these issues.

Paperback ISBN: 978-0-9964464-4-0
Kindle ISBN: 978-0-9964464-5-7
EPUB ISBN: 978-0-9964464-6-4

www.PrestonLoveJr.com

www.ingramcontent.com/pod-product-compliance
Lightning Source LLC
Chambersburg PA
CBHW030558270326
41927CB00007B/973